CW00808886

BRITISH WILDLIFE PHOTOGRAPHY AWARDS

COLLECTION 2

Managing Editor: Paul Mitchell
Senior Editor: Donna Wood
Senior Designer: Tracey Butler
Image retouching and colour repro: Jacqueline Street
Production: Lorraine Taylor
Indexer: Hilary Bird

Produced by AA Publishing
© AA Media Limited 2011
Reprinted October 2014

Published by AA Publishing (a trading name of AA Media Limited, whose registered
office is Fanum House, Basing View, Basingstoke RG21 4EA; registered number
06112600).

A05296

ISBN: 978-0-7495-7115-3

A CIP catalogue record for this book is available from the British Library.

The contents of this book are believed correct at the time of printing. Nevertheless,
the publishers cannot be held responsible for any errors or omissions or for changes
in the details given in this book or for the consequences of any reliance on the
information provided by the same. This does not affect your statutory rights.

Caption information has been supplied by the photographers and the publishers
accept no responsibility for errors or omissions in the details given.

Printed and bound in Italy by Printer Trento SRL
theAA.com/shop

ANDY ROUSE/2020VISION >   HIGHLY COMMENDED

Wild Boar Sniffing
(Wild Boar, *Sus scrofa*)
Monmouthshire, Wales
See page 30

CONTENTS

ROSS HODDINOTT >

Thick-legged Flower Beetle on Corn Marigold
(Thick-legged Flower Beetle, *Oedemera nobilis*)
Pentire Point, near Newquay, Cornwall, England
See page 176

THE BRITISH WILDLIFE PHOTOGRAPHY AWARDS

MAGGIE GOWAN
BWPA DIRECTOR

BRITISH WILDLIFE PHOTOGRAPHY AWARDS

The British Wildlife Photography Awards were established to recognise the talents of photographers practicing in Britain, while at the same time highlighting the great wealth and diversity of Britain's natural history. The driving motivation to set up the Awards evolved through the nation's growing awareness of the local environment and the need for its protection. With a nationwide touring exhibition of the best entries, the Awards aim to:

- celebrate British wildlife, in all its beauty and diversity, through a collection of inspirational photographs
- recognise the talents of photographers (of all nationalities) practising in Britain
- showcase the very best of British nature photography to a wide audience
- engage all ages with evocative and powerful imagery
- raise awareness about British biodiversity, species and habitats

For further information about the annual competition and touring exhibition, please visit **www.bwpawards.co.uk**

A MESSAGE FROM RICHARD BENYON MP

Minister for Natural Environment and Fisheries

This collection of stunning photography from all over the UK provides a unique and beautiful insight into many of our British species, and proves it is not necessary to travel internationally in order to take creative and imaginative pictures of wildlife.

The exclusively British wildlife subjects illustrated in this book show how privileged we are to have such wonderful and diverse flora and fauna.

Defra is fully supportive of this acclaimed initiative and congratulates all the winning photographers and those featured in this book.

With two special awards for young people, I hope this showcase will inspire all ages to explore and discover our wonderful natural heritage and capture their own images.

THE CATEGORIES

1. Animal Portraits

Images that capture the character or spirit of the subject in an imaginative way, giving a sense of the animal's 'personality'.

2. Animal Behaviour

Entries showing unusual or remarkable behaviour in an original and compelling composition, especially those showing the judges something they don't know or haven't seen before.

3. Urban Wildlife

Increasingly, wildlife can be found in our towns and cities. In this category, we were looking for an original image that shows animal adaptation to urban environments.

4. Hidden Britain

Revealing the secret universe that is life in the undergrowth – a life that is all around us but rarely seen.

5. Coast and Marine

Imaginative photographs that reveal the behaviour of marine animals or create a sense of place or occasion. This includes marine animals near the sea, underwater, at the sea shore and within the coastal zone.

6. Wildlife in My Backyard

Gardens represent a vital habitat for some of our most threatened species. In this category we were looking for stunning photos of animals in the garden, backyard, balcony, or any space where you or your friends or family do something to encourage wildlife.

7. Habitat

Animals in their environment and plants and their partners. Original images portraying the relationship between wildlife and its environment.

8. British Seasons

A portfolio of four images portraying British wildlife at its best in each of the four seasons; or a portfolio of four from just one season. Each image should capture the essence of the season along with the wildlife subject.

9. Living Landscape: Connectivity

Being connected to the natural world is good for our health, our happiness and for the future. It is The Wildlife Trusts' vision to create a resilient environment, rich in wildlife and great for people, called a 'Living Landscape'. This category was purposely left open to interpretation to encourage fresh and imaginative responses. Connectivity might be physical, sensory, seasonal or otherwise. Positive images illustrating how habitats, species, communities and individuals interconnect within rural and urban settings, were encouraged.

10. Documentary Series

A sequence of up to six images on any British wildlife, conservation or environmental issue, showing innovation in storytelling.

11. Wildlife on Video

An inspirational and dynamic sequence (up to a minute long) illustrating the unique power of video as a medium for capturing British wildlife. Some stills from the film are featured in this book. The whole film and commended entries can be viewed at www.bwpawards.co.uk

12. *Outdoor Photography* Editor's Choice

Each month the competition was running, the editor of *Outdoor Photography* chose an image for future publication in the magazine.

13. Young British Wildlife Photographers

There were two age ranges in this category; up to 11 years and 12 to 18 years. There were no specific subjects; we were looking for striking and memorable images of any British wildlife species.

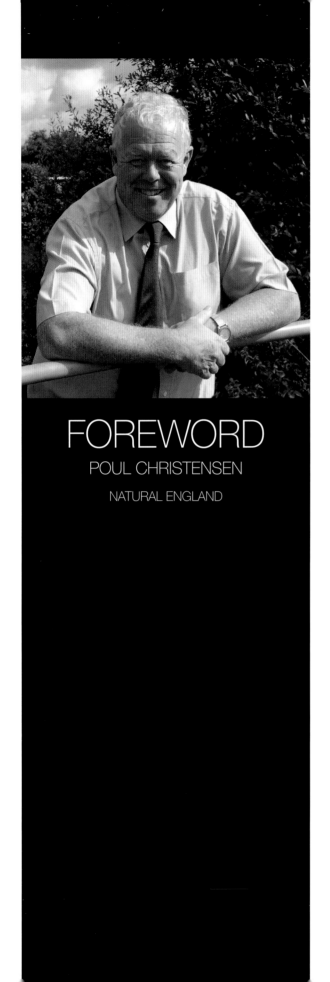

FOREWORD

POUL CHRISTENSEN

NATURAL ENGLAND

Welcome to a second inspirational collection from the finalists of the British Wildlife Photography Awards.

We have a wealth and diversity of wildlife in the British Isles; charismatic and surprising species that share our land and seas. These images have perfectly captured the best of British wildlife – and, whether commonplace or seldom-seen, this collection reminds us that all life matters.

This competition throws a spotlight on the challenges our environment faces. The losses and steep declines faced by British wildlife have never been so acute and, looking at these images, it is impossible not to feel a sense of responsibility. Co-ordinated action, raised awareness and enjoyment of our flora and fauna are fundamental to the survival of our natural heritage. I am especially heartened by the pictures from eight-year old Walter Lovell and 16-year old Oliver Wilks – the early steps, I hope, on lifelong journeys of discovery.

I would also like to thank the thousands of people who submitted photographs. People from all walks of life and from every corner of the country have shared their favourite images, resulting in an extremely high-quality final selection. I look forward to seeing this competition go from strength to strength.

I hope that the images in this book inspire people to explore Britain's wild places for themselves – garden or village green; coast or countryside; mountain, moor or down – there is a fascinating world of wildlife out there for you to discover.

Poul Christensen
Chair, Natural England

ALEXANDER MUSTARD/2020VISION >
HIGHLY COMMENDED

Toad in the Hole
(Common Toad, *Bufo bufo*)
River Orchy, Highlands, Scotland
See page 161

INTRODUCTION

NICK BAKER

NATURALIST AND BROADCASTER

It's a brilliant world out there and our relationship with the thin crust of life that coats its surface starts right here, on our own patch. This is where intimacy with nature is at its most intense and personal. What is important to keep in mind as you let your eyes roll over this fine array of images is where they all come from – right here in Britain.

This second collection of home-grown productions destroys the myth that to be a member of this seemingly exclusive bunch of individuals known as wildlife photographers you need to spend gazillions on kit, have a massive travel budget and be a fully paid up 'wildlifer'.

Flick through the pages of this book and you feel as though you've entered some kind of wildlife fantasia where there's a plethora of perfected form, vibrant and exhilarating colour, and a wealth of extraordinary behaviours, all documented by a cunning, patient and dedicated clan; the photographers. While I don't claim to be among their number yet, I feel that because I've had a go I can at least understand them a little and appreciate the magic that each of these stunning frames represents – the countless hours waiting, the technology, the planning, and the often overlooked but vital ingredient to many award-winning shots; a smidgen of luck, a fleeting moment of good fortune captured for eternity by the timely opening of a shutter.

It's this last variable that makes for a startling and original photo, and one further advantage to photographing what's close to hand is that often to get the image you want you need to know your subject; whether it's the way the light falls or the subtle nuances of an animal's behaviour. Where in the world but on your own patch are the odds shortened enough for this to happen?

This second collection of wildlife images proves that to know your subject means you can commence the dance of fortune with lady luck and stand a chance of getting the image you desire.

Part of my recent work has involved observing a rare bird, the Ring Ouzel, for the RSPB as well as taking families on wildlife-watching courses for the Field Studies Council. In carrying out these assignments I've realised just how disinterested we have become; how disconnected and divorced from the land and environment that surround us. While this is not the place to analyse why this may be, I would like to draw attention to the role that photographers have in turning this around.

'This collection is a truly in

This collection is a truly inspiring one. It shows us what we have; how rich we are as a group of islands. The images compel those that view them to look deeper, look closer, and appreciate the subtleties of the natural world around us. They give it value, and the basis of conservation is appreciation. How can we preserve and conserve an orchid or a butterfly, or for that matter, something just as beautiful to a wildlife photographer (let's say a slug or pseudoscorpion) if we don't even know they are out there?

These images open our eyes to the wonders of our own biodiversity, not just the well-loved wildlife in our prime and protected nature reserves, but the common species that share our own immediate patch, perched in our gardens, sliming over our doorsteps or eating our petunias. All have their beauty, their form and their function.

The rules to this competition are that there are none – other than where your subject is based geographically. Your pass card for this exclusive club is no more than focus (in more than one way) and an imaginative and curious eye. These photographs make me wish I had achieved similar greatness, but they don't make me want to quit trying and stamp on my flash cards. Instead they inspire me to persevere, to look deeper and see the true texture of the web of life in which we are directly suspended. I hope this collection has the same effect on you.

So do enjoy the best of British – its wildlife and its photographers.

Nick Baker
Dartmoor, July 2011
(Photograph of Nick Baker courtesy of Dorling Kindersley)

DAVE PRESSLAND

Speckled Bush-cricket nymph
(Speckled Bush-cricket nymph, *Leptophyes punctatissima*)
Belvedere, Kent, England
See page 110

Canon

The British Wildlife Photography Awards 2011-2012 are held in association with Canon. Canon is a world leader in imaging products and solutions for the digital home and office.

Canon are passionate about providing consumers with imaging solutions that empower creativity and innovation. They offer the largest and broadest end-to-end range of imaging products from cameras, camcorders, binoculars and personal printers to large format printers, digital radiography systems, digital retina cameras and professional digital printing presses and Canon is regularly recognised by industry bodies for its product innovation and quality.

To learn more about Canon products, please visit Canon's website:
www.canon.co.uk

Scottish Natural Heritage

Scottish Natural Heritage is the government's adviser on all aspects of nature and landscape across Scotland. Their role is to help everyone understand, value and enjoy Scotland's nature now and in the future. For further information visit:
www.snh.gov.uk

Countryside Council for Wales

The Countryside Council for Wales is the government's statutory advisor on sustaining natural beauty, wildlife and the opportunity for outdoor enjoyment in Wales and its inshore waters. CCW champions the environment and landscapes of Wales and its coastal waters as sources of natural and cultural riches, as a foundation for economic and social activity, and as a place for leisure and learning opportunities. CCW aims to make the environment a valued part of everyone's life in Wales.
www.ccw.gov.uk

a million voices for nature

RSPB

The RSPB speaks out for birds and wildlife, tackling the problems that threaten our environment. With over a million members, it is a powerful voice for nature.

www.rspb.org.uk

WWF

WWF is building a future where people and nature thrive together. That's why WWF is as passionate about tackling global climate change, and finding ways to share the planet's resources more sustainably, as it is about protecting endangered wildlife.

www.wwf.org.uk

The Wildlife Trusts

The Wildlife Trusts comprise 47 local Wildlife Trusts covering the whole of the UK, with more than 800,000 members. Collectively they manage thousands of nature reserves and run marine conservation projects around the coast. The Wildlife Trusts also advise landowners on wildlife-friendly land management, and every year work with thousands of schools.

www.wildlifetrusts.org

Buglife

Buglife is a registered charity and the only organisation in Europe devoted to the conservation of all invertebrates – everything from bees to beetles, woodlice to worms and jumping spiders to jellyfish! Invertebrates are vital for the health of the planet. They pollinate our crops and wildflowers, recycle nutrients back into the ground, and are a vital source of food for other animals such as birds and mammals. The food we eat, the fish we catch, the birds we see, the flowers we smell and the hum of life we hear simply would not exist without wonderful, amazing, fascinating bugs.

www.buglife.org.uk

Countryside Jobs Service

Countryside Jobs Service is a small ethically focused company providing information on countryside careers including jobs, volunteers, professional training and more. Established in July 1994, CJS is run by a small, dedicated team of ex-rangers, smallholders and ecologists working on a co-operative basis to ensure they publish the widest range of relevant information for readers.

www.countryside-jobs.com

***Outdoor Photography* Magazine**

Outdoor Photography's intriguing balance of features, tests, techniques, travel and conservation stories make it the most relevant magazine in the dynamic world of nature photography. Each issue features an inspiring array of landscape, wildlife and travel features, with regular, intelligent contributions by leading nature photographers from around the world.

www.thegmcgroup.com

WildlifeXpo

WildlifeXpo is the UK's most comprehensive wildlife exhibition where all things wildlife can be found under one roof. WildlifeXpo highlights wildlife and conservation issues and promotes wildlife watching as a means to conservation.

WildlifeXpo provides opportunities to listen to lectures and presentations, and to meet some of the Britain's best-known wildlife presenters, view award-winning wildlife photography and participate in workshops with photography experts.

You will find specialist wildlife travel companies, binocular and camera specialists, outdoor clothing, wildlife art, wildlife and conservation charities and much, much more. WildlifeXpo is run in support of wildlife charities.

www.wildlifexpo.com

***Wildlife Extra* – the web's wildlife magazine**

Wildlife Extra is for people who like watching, conserving and photographing wildlife and hearing the latest wildlife news.

Wildlife Extra brings you a guide to UK nature reserves and National Parks, a selection of wildlife and conservation jobs, lets you know the best places to watch whales or go on a safari holiday and provides wildlife photography tips, competitions and articles. Free subscription.

www.wildlifeextra.com

Inspiring Creativity

Serif

Serif develops and publishes award-winning, affordable, accessible and creative software, which has already inspired over six million customers worldwide. With more than 20 years of operating history and over 200 independent awards, Serif has enabled businesses, educational establishments and ordinary PC users to achieve professional-quality results – whatever their level of experience.
www.serif.com

www.genesis-digital.net

Genesis Imaging

Genesis Imaging is proud to produce images for the British Wildlife Photography Awards and its nationwide touring exhibition. Genesis offers a full range of photographic printing and finishing services – from Giclée and Lambda printing to über-trendy Perspex Face Mounting and bespoke framing and much more, all under one roof. Their superb fine art prints have graced the walls of famous galleries from the National Portrait Gallery to New York's Museum of Modern Art.
www.genesis-digital.net

▲towergate camerasure

Towergate Camerasure

Towergate Camerasure is the leading provider of insurance for the Photographic, Video and Multimedia Industry. With over 20 years experience, Towergate Camerasure has developed insurance solutions that are flexible enough to meet the individual requirements of the professional, semi professional and keen enthusiast. Towergate Camerasure makes insurance easy, with friendly, knowledgeable staff and a fast and efficient claims service.
www.towergatecamerasure.co.uk

THE JUDGES

Paul Wilkinson

Head of Living Landscape
The Wildlife Trusts

Paul leads The Wildlife Trusts' vision to create A Living Landscape, which has the restoration of the natural environment at its heart. Paul's interest in wildlife photography was rekindled through this recovery plan for nature, championed since 2006, to create a resilient and healthy environment, rich in wildlife. Paul previously worked as the Director of Regional Policy for The Wildlife Trusts in the East of England, during which time he was a member of the East of England Regional Assembly and chaired the region's Biodiversity Forum for six years. Paul is a member of the Institute of Ecology and Environmental Management.

Ben Osborne

Wildlife and Landscape
Photographer

Ben has been a freelance photographer for 25 years. He has worked on all seven continents but is best known for his images of Antarctica in the book of the BBC series *Life in the Freezer*. His work has been published in numerous magazines including *National Geographic, BBC Wildlife, Geo, Radio Times* and *Hello!* In 2007 he was overall winner of the Shell Wildlife Photographer of the Year competition and won the Creative Visions of Nature category. His work was recognised by the Royal Photographic Society in 2008 through the award of an honorary fellowship. Ben divides his time between travelling the world on assignments, leading workshops in the UK and abroad, touring with audio-visual presentations and working on collaborative arts projects around the UK.

Sue Herdman

Editor of *National Trust Magazine*

Sue is the editor of *National Trust Magazine*, a title renowned for its use of beautiful photography and for the size of its audience: it currently holds the fourth highest magazine circulation figure in the UK, with a readership of some 3.8 million. Throughout her career Sue has worked with photographers to capture arresting images to accompany features, from those on China and its Great Wall, to the Mexican home of artist Frida Kahlo, behind-the-scenes on films and television series and on to the sublime landscapes of pastoral England. She has written for broadsheets including *The Daily Telegraph, The Sunday Telegraph, The Times* and the *Guardian* and, prior to her current role, was a features and commissioning editor at BBC Worldwide Magazines.

Paul Mitchell

Managing Editor
AA Publishing

Paul has been at AA Publishing since 2005, becoming managing editor in 2007 following two years in the travel editorial department. He is keen to build on AA Publishing's position as one of Britain's foremost travel and leisure publishers, and its growing reputation in publishing best-selling photographic titles. The addition of the British Wildlife Photography Awards to its publishing portfolio in 2010 was a key development, reinforcing the commitment to publishing books of the highest photographic calibre, and showcasing the very best of Britain and its wonderfully diverse natural environment.

David Fidler

**Pro Imaging Account Manager
Canon UK**

David has worked in both the commercial and retail sections of the photographic industry for over 12 years, and for the past seven years he has worked for Canon UK Ltd as their Professional Imaging Account Manager. Within this role, he is responsible for driving business in the nature and wildlife market and working with some of the UK's top photographers.

Mark Ward

**Editor
RSPB *Birds* Magazine**

Mark is the editor of the RSPB's *Birds* magazine. He has been writing about birds and nature from a young age   his first feature appeared in *Birdwatch* magazine when he was 15. Mark has enthused many people about wildlife through his writing in titles including *Bird Watching, Natural World* and *Country Walking*; his newspaper columns, and books including *Bird Identification and Fieldcraft: A Birdwatcher's Guide*. Passionate about nature, his ambition is to see as many species of wildlife in the UK as possible in his lifetime.

Tom Hind

**European Head of Content
Getty Images**

Tom has worked as European Head of Content for Getty Images for the last five years, a role which involves creating imagery for Getty's house collections and managing European Art Direction. Before that he worked as Head of Art Buying for WWAV Rapp Collins for seven years, commissioning photography assignments for diverse clients such as Sony, LTSB and Friends of the Earth.

Steve Watkins

**Editor
Outdoor Photography Magazine**

Steve is an award-winning travel photographer and writer, and editor of *Outdoor Photography* magazine. He wrote and shot three of the titles in the internationally bestselling 'Unforgettable' series, including *Unforgettable Things to Do Before you Die*. Steve has walked on the wild side for more than 20 years as an adventurer and travel photographer, and in the past eight years he shot 120,000 images in 65 countries.

THE JUDGES

Greg Armfield

**Photographic and Film Manager
WWF-UK**

Greg is photographic and film manager for WWF-UK. He has worked in the photographic industry for over 10 years, combining both the NGO sector (National Trust and WWF) and private sector (Emap and Construction Photography). Greg has worked in all facets of the industry, from artistic director at Construction Photography to photographer, editor and commissioner. Has worked for WWF for the last five years, originally heading up the photographic department but now also leading on film, with responsibility for all photo commissions.

Patrick Llewellyn

**Picture Editor
*Ink Publishing***

After studying art at Camberwell, engineering and product design at UCE and psychology at the University of London, Patrick embarked on a career in the world of print journalism. He learnt his trade freelancing as a picture researcher on some of the leading newspaper titles including *The Independent, The Sun and The Times*. He was the deputy picture editor at *The Sunday Times Magazine* from 2004 to early 2011. He is now the picture editor at Ink Publishing, working across a diverse range of titles. Patrick works closely with the world's top photographic agencies, commissioning some of the finest reportage, art and portrait photographers working today.

Steve Young

Wildlife Photographer

Proving a popular winner of last year's BWPA competition with his photograph *Herring Gull in Wave*, Steve is the 2010 British Wildlife Photographer of the Year. One of the UK's top bird photographers and a columnist for both *Birdwatch* and *Outdoor Photography* magazines, Steve is also the author of two books: *Essential Guide to Bird Photography* and *A Field Guide to Bird Photography*.

WITH THANKS TO

All the photographers who have participated in the awards

The sponsors and supporters

The judges

AA Publishing

Midas Public Relations

Natural England

The National Trust and these properties:

Calke Abbey, Derbyshire

Nunnington Hall, Yorkshire

Trelissick Gallery, Cornwall

Penrhyn Castle, North Wales

Alexandra Palace

Horniman Museum

Nature in Art

Moors Valley Country Park

The National Trust for Scotland

Youth Hostel Association

British Society of Underwater Photographers

Made By Hippo Ltd

Picture This

Pinkeye Graphics

Matthew Chatfield

Carl Crawley

Rich Tribe

Ralph Tribe

Clare Webb

Victoria Skeet

Emma Louise Clarke

Chris Hart

Katie Ackerman

Kate Foreshew

Claire Harris

Jennie Hart

Charlotte Salaman

Babs Gowan

Rebecca Blanchard

Deborah Ishihara

David Johnson

BRITISH WILDLIFE
PHOTOGRAPHER OF THE YEAR

BRITISH WILDLIFE PHOTOGRAPHER OF THE YEAR 2011

OVERALL WINNER

RICHARD SHUCKSMITH >

Jellyfish in the Blue Sea of Sula Sgeir
(Jellyfish, *Pelegia noctiluca*)
Off Sula Sgeir, Scotland

Living on a boat, the MV *Halton,* and diving off some of the remote islands off the west coast of Scotland is an exhilarating experience. Sula Sgeir (meaning Gannet Rock) is 41 miles north of the Butt of Lewis. These wild and exposed islands provide habitat for an astounding variety of marine life. Places like these feel all the more special because although remote and difficult to get to, they are a part of our heritage.

JUDGE'S CHOICE: GREG ARMFIELD, *WWF*
'A truly beautiful shot of a jellyfish that perfectly captures its iridescent colours and magical qualities. All the more remarkable that it exists in UK waters. Fantastic.'

JUDGE'S CHOICE: DAVID FIDLER, *CANON*
'This stunning image of a jellyfish off the UK coast is truly amazing. Firstly, the striking composition and beautiful colours really draw you into the image. Secondly, the thought that this creature lives off our shores highlights the variety and range of species we have in the UK.'

ANIMAL
PORTRAITS

ANIMAL PORTRAITS WINNER

MARK SMITH

Mystical Mist
(Fallow Deer, *Dama dama*)
Richmond, Surrey, England

I love photographing deer in the autumn and a forecast
of mist just makes me even more eager to get out
photographing them. I heard this deer before I saw
it and using the mist and wind direction as cover I
managed to get in place with tripod set up before he
knew I was there. I was able to get a few shots before
he slowly ambled off into the mist in the background.

JUDGE'S CHOICE: SUE HERDMAN, *NATIONAL TRUST MAGAZINE*

'There was unanimous consent when this image came
up on screen at the judging: it was a photograph of
star quality. Captured on lens was a scene that, with its
colour palette and composition, held something close to
that created by the brush of the Victorian painter Edwin
Landseer in his Monarch of the Glen. The photograph
has a painterly feel: romantic, still, majestic and, with
the direct gaze of animal to lens, a rare intimacy caught
on camera.'

ANDY ROUSE   HIGHLY COMMENDED

Little Owl Backlit
(Little Owl, *Athene noctua)*
Wales

Last summer I worked on a unique group of Little Owls that were nesting
in an old stone wall. It was a wonderful experience. This image shows one
of the parents chilling out on the wall. I managed to back my car slowly
against the wall to get the angle against the setting sun.

GRAHAM EATON   HIGHLY COMMENDED

Mute Swan
(Mute Swan, *Cygnus olor*)
Llyn Padarn, Llanberis, Wales

I was photographing a Mute Swan in split level, to show the whole bird
rather than the half we usually see. This one particular swan kept looking at
its reflection in the dome port on my underwater housing. It was reaching
towards its reflection when I got this shot. I like the strong eye contact and
the exaggerated length of its neck, due to the wide-angle lens.

MARK SMITH   HIGHLY COMMENDED

Swooping Kite
(Red Kite, *Milvus milvus*)
Rhayader, Powys, Wales

For me, kites are one of the most acrobatic raptors in the UK. No other bird
seems to glide and then twirl into a spiral before cruising out again in a
leisurely fashion as if nothing energetic or spectacular had happened – as
if they are doing it just for fun. This is something that I really wanted to
capture in as intimate a way as possible.

ANDY ROUSE/2020VISION <

HIGHLY COMMENDED

Wild Boar Sniffing

(Wild Boar, *Sus scrofa*)

Monmouthshire, Wales

As part of the 2020VISION project I am working on, I came across this wild boar sleeping one day, so I laid down in the bracken and waited. When she woke up she knew I was there but the wind did not allow her to smell me, so she sniffed more, hence the image.

STEWARD ELLETT > HIGHLY COMMENDED

Windy Day

(Red Squirrel, *Sciurrus vulgaris*)

Formby Point, Merseyside, England

At Formby Point the Red Squirrel is quite used to seeing people, which helps when trying to get some photographs. Even though it was a very windy day I found a suitable spot to set up my camera and with the help of a few nuts this Red Squirrel obliged, spending a few minutes eating and grooming. The wind made this shot special, especially as he had really nice ear tufts.

RON COULTER   HIGHLY COMMENDED

Golden Eagle
(Golden Eagle, *Aquila chrysaetos*)
Near Aviemore, Scotland

It was midwinter with continuous snow when I hiked up the hills
of Aviemore.

The eagle is captive.

MATTHEW WATKINSON   HIGHLY COMMENDED

Gribun Otter
(European Otter, *Lutra lutra*)
Gribun Cliffs, Isle of Mull, Scotland

Having found this otter, my approach technique involved mad *It's a Knockout*-style sprinting across the shoreline boulders each time he dove, making sure I didn't break my legs and that I was intimately hugging a rock every time he resurfaced. Eventually I was close enough to take a nice picture with my budget camera equipment. I reckon it worked as well!

MARK SMITH   HIGHLY COMMENDED

Little Big Eyes
(Grey Seal, *Halichoerus grypus*)
Lincolnshire, England

It was my birthday and I'd been planning a trip to photograph the seals
for months. It snowed really hard for a week and most of the country was
grinding to a halt. You really have to know what you're doing to get this
close; it has to be 100 percent on their terms. After searching for a weaned
pup that was confident on its own, I lay on my front for around 30 minutes,
slowly approaching inch by inch. By the time I was close the pup did the
rest; he was as interested in my lens hood as I was in photographing him in
the snow. A hugely rewarding experience and one I'll treasure.

LEE FISHER   HIGHLY COMMENDED

Cobweb Kingfisher
(Kingfisher, *Alcedo atthis*)
Worcestershire, England

This preferred Kingfisher perch is always full of cobwebs in the early
mornings. It took quite a while to capture the bird in the right pose and
position, but after numerous attempts everything came together.

Home Sweet Home

(Water Vole, *Arvicola amphibius*)
Matlock, Derbyshire, England

There are a few popular locations where you can photograph Water Voles, but I really wanted to capture them in a more natural setting. When I came across this spot, I knew it would lend itself to the imagination of 'Ratty', the character from the children's fairytale *The Wind in The Willows*. This enchanting little fellow looked right at home. He busily tidied his home as if for visitors. Maybe Mole was coming to tea?

BRIAN CHARD　　　　　　HIGHLY COMMENDED

Red Deer in Blizzard
(Red Deer, *Cervus elaphus*)
Newtonmore, Inverness-shire, Scotland

The snow worked for us in that it brought the deer down from the hills, but it caused problems with focusing; snow being blown onto the front of lens and the normal exposure issues. We shot from the vehicle, most of the time using beanbags. This shot was taken as we were leaving. It was approaching blizzard conditions. I had seen a small group fairly close to the track, enabling me to fill the frame with a portrait shot.

Soaking Wet Starling
(Starling, *Sturnus vulgaris*)
Rainford, Merseyside, England

This image was taken during a dry spell of weather in May 2011. Most birds were highly appreciative of the water source in my garden for drinking and occasionally bathing. The starlings soon found the water and would regularly take a bath together. The difficulty I had in taking this picture was to isolate just one bird and to ensure the camera had focussed on the subject and not the water splashes in front of the bird.

TONY MOSS

New Forest Badger Cub
(Eurasian Badger, *Meles meles*)
New Forest, Hampshire, England

I've been watching this sett for many years and in the past photographing cubs has always been a challenge, due mainly to the vigorous growth of the surrounding bracken. The recent dry spring has delayed bracken growth in the forest and on this particular evening everything came together; fantastic soft evening light and a very co-operative badger cub.

RON McCOMBE

Brown Hare
(Brown Hare, *Lepus europaeus*)
Fogo, Nr Kelso, Roxburghshire, Scotland

It was the end of a nice sunny day and the light was fading fast. I was watching brown hares in a wheat field that was being harvested. The hares were scurrying around as the tractors went about their business. I noticed a brown hare on the left-hand side coming towards me along the hedgerow. It stopped briefly and I managed to get the picture before it moved off.

JAMIE HALL

Short-Eared Owl in Snow

(Short-Eared Owl, *Asio flammeus*)
North Lincolnshire, England

After a four-and-a-half hour drive through heavy snowfall I found myself in the middle of the the North Lincolnshire countryside. The only company I had was in the form of this Short-Eared Owl, which despite the awful conditions was still gliding over the snow-filled meadows and successfully on two occasions managing to somehow catch its prey by listening to vibrations and dive-bombing into the thick snow.

MARK SISSON <

Mute Swan Cygnet Swimming in Canal
(Mute Swan, *Cygnus olor*)
Newport, Shropshire, England

The family of Mute Swans who nest on the canal in my home town are in many ways local celebrities, so last summer I spent several evenings sitting in the canal to habituate them to my presence there alongside the usual fishermen and gain their trust. The young cygnets were increasingly nosey, swimming up to me to stare down my water-level lens.

JACKY PARKER ʌ

Mute Swan and Cygnet Sleeping
(Mute Swan, *Cygnus olor*)
Abbotsbury Swannery, Dorset, England

After several hours of walking amongst these beautiful creatures at Abbotsbury Swannery in Dorset I was drawn to this particular swan with a cygnet on her back, which appeared to be quite tired. I waited patiently for it to fall asleep, and as it did, to my surprise the adult swan placed her head on top of the cygnet, which was absolutely adorable and to me summed up motherhood.

WILL ATKINS

Male Green Lizard on Gorse
(Western Green Lizard, *Lacerta bilineata*)
Bournemouth, Dorset, England

Native to continental Europe, green lizards are now established on the cliffs of Dorset, the recent warm summers favouring incubation of their eggs. This adult male had selected a vantage point in a flowering gorse bush to look for a mate, from where he allowed a close approach as we made our way to the beach below for some sun worshipping of our own.

TERRY WHITTAKER/2020VISION <

Young Pine Marten
(Pine Marten, *Martes martes*)
Black Isle, Scotland

I worked with a family of Pine Martens over a period of several weeks, slowly gaining the confidence of the female. Eventually she started to bring her large kits out into the open. After eating the food I left out for them, the kits would often play in front of my hide, rolling and tumbling in the heather and dashing up and down trees.

ANDREW PARKINSON ∧

Great Crested Grebe with a Fish
(Great Crested Grebe, *Podiceps cristatus*)
Derbyshire, England

I had been photographing some coots when this grebe suddenly popped up in front of me with a fish. I immediately knew that I wanted to shoot it in portrait format to include its reflection, but I could tell from its body shape that it was preparing to dive, so I decided that an imperfect something was better than a perfect nothing.

JULES COX <

Strike a Pose!
(Red Squirrel, *Sciurus vulgaris*)
Cairngorms National Park, Scotland

I took this image in the Cairngorms in January this year. I have been visiting this particular feeding site for a number of years now. Red Squirrels have to be one of my favourite British mammals. They look especially beautiful in winter with their striking ear tufts. This was my favourite shot of the three days I spent photographing them. I love the way it shows their playful characters. This particular plucky fellow struck this pose for a fraction of a second, just long enough for me to get the shot. A miracle in itself as I was laughing so much at the time.

JOANNA DAVIES >

Harvest Mouse
(Harvest Mouse, *Micromys minutus*)
Southampton, England

Harvest mice, Britain's smallest rodent and seen by few photographers, have always intrigued me, and when I heard of the opportunity to photograph them I jumped at the chance and flew down for the day. The real challenge was the sheer speed they moved, far faster than I had imagined. After ages of waiting for that elusive shot, the mouse quickly made eye contact with the lens before scampering off again.

Photographed in captivity.

DES ONG

Alien View
(Orange-tip Butterfly, *Anthocharis cardamines*)
Loughborough, Leicestershire, England

Orange-tip Butterflies have been visiting our garden for the past couple of years. My focus this time was to capture an abstract, close-up, 'alien' view of its fascinating features that are impossible to see with a casual glance. The simple composition was key to providing the intrigue. In addition to this headshot, I have also taken some beautiful, painterly images depicting the delicate texture of its patterned wings.

RICHARD PACKWOOD

Dipper Looking Towards Nest
(Dipper, *Cinclus cinclus*)
Powys, Mid Wales

Dippers regularly nest in my own-design predator-proof
nestbox under a bridge in the garden. The site is very
dark, which necessitated fill flash to match the brightly
lit background on the far side of the bridge. By keeping
a low viewpoint the reflection of this background
carpeted the water under the bridge.

JULES COX

Vole Reflection
(Water Vole, *Arvicola amphibious*)
Kent, England

I spent several days at the start of last winter photographing Water Voles at this re-introduction site. Achieving this low level reflection shot involved a lot of patience, sitting prone and perfectly still in icy cold water wearing chest waders for hours and hours on end, in the hope that a vole might happen by. Once I had a vole in front of me, I couldn't move a muscle, otherwise they're gone in the blink of an eye. To add to the challenge, you're also working with your camera gear a matter of centimetres off the water's surface. In my experience, cameras and water don't mix that well!

STEVE ROUND

Common Toad Photographed at Low Level
with Reflection of Reedbed Creating a Golden Glow
(Common Toad, *Bufo bufo*)
Clwyd, North Wales

Having photographed the toads which had been making their way to a
small lake throughout the afternoon, I was looking for some new ideas
for shots. The last sunlight of the day lit up the reedbed, giving a lovely
warm-coloured reflection to the water. I lay on the ground to get as low as
possible and waited for a toad to appear on the surface. This one was in
the perfect spot, away from floating vegetation, giving a nice clean image.

MATT BINSTEAD

Red Fox
(Red Fox, *Vulpes vulpes*)
British Wildlife Centre, Lingfield, Surrey, England

Working closely with wild animals allows you to build a bond and mutual trust. This in turn allows you to get closer to them than you ever could in the wild, opening up new opportunities in photography. This photograph is taken from a low viewpoint with a wide-angle lens to emphasize the movement and closeness of the fox bearing down on you, while still maintaining the natural background.

BRETT LEWIS ∧

Grass Snake
(Grass Snake, *Natrix natrix*)
Lickey Hills Country Park, West Midlands, England

As an ecologist, one of my favourite subjects is British herpetofauna. I visited a country park and asked the wardens if they knew of the best spots to observe and photograph reptiles and amphibians. Their knowledge was invaluable and I found this large female Grass Snake on a woodpile exactly where they said she would be. After shooting with my DSLR for a short while I used my compact to give a much greater depth of field to include the environment she was in.

MARK DARLINGTON >

Tentative Wood Mouse Stealing Corn
(Wood Mouse, *Apodemus sylvaticus*)
Derbyshire, England

Always carrying a Canon S90 with me, I noticed mice fetching and hiding corn. They paused to eat pieces of maze. Completely oblivious to my presence, one mouse allowed me within feet. In slow motion it stretched to gather maze I had sprinkled around my outstretched arm with the S90 in hand.

ANIMAL
BEHAVIOUR

ANIMAL BEHAVIOUR WINNER

ANDREW PARKINSON

Grey Heron Walking on Water
(Grey Heron, *Ardea cinerea*)
Derbyshire, England

It was dawn at a secluded fishing lake when this heron suddenly plunged, osprey-like into the middle of the lake, emerging moments later with a fish. This image captures the moment that it powered out of the water and took flight.

MARK HAMBLIN   HIGHLY COMMENDED

Otter – Female and Cub Drying Coats
(European Otter, *Lutra lutra*)
Eetlar, Shetlands, Scotland

Working with otter expert Brydon Thomason from Shetland Nature,
I followed the activity of this female otter and her cub for over an hour,
waiting for an opportunity to get close to the water's edge where I could
get a shot. Anticipating where they would come ashore, I got myself into
position lying prone on a rock and captured the moment that they shook
themselves dry.

ANDREW PARKINSON   HIGHLY COMMENDED

Coot in Hot Pursuit
(Coot, *Fulica atra*)
Derbyshire, England

I love trying to produce something different with familiar or oft overlooked subjects and coots are certainly one of those birds. Working in the last few moments of glancing evening sunlight I was able to backlight this territorial pursuit and to reveal how beautiful and engaging these birds really are.

WENDY BALL   HIGHLY COMMENDED

A Gannet Trying to Land in High Wind
(Northern Gannet, *Morus bassanus*)
Bempton Cliffs, Flamborough Head, Yorkshire, England

It was a blustery day on the cliff top. I observed that in order to land,
the gannets were hovering at the cliff edge and 'backing in' to a suitable
landing space on the crowded cliff face. This required fine tuning of their
wings in order to be accurate and to avoid the awaiting sharp beaks!

JOHN OLIVER HIGHLY COMMENDED

Orange-Tip Butterflies Mating
(Orange-Tip Butterfly, *Anthocharis Cardamines*)
Stanley, Near Perth, Perthshire

It was a sunny day in early May and there were a few Orange-Tips flying around. Having followed this pair for about 20 minutes, photographing them in the grass, the female landed on a tree which gave me the opportunity to show proper dimension and separation between them because they were now at eye level. I took three shots before they flew off.

JUDGE'S CHOICE: MARK WARD, *RSPB* BIRDS *MAGAZINE*

'Butterflies are the photographer's friends as they bask in the sun in all their colourful glory, but John's portrait caught my eye because it captures a rarely portrayed, intimate moment in their short life-cycle. Beautiful composition, a focus on the easily overlooked female Orange-Tip and the sense of anticipation from the waiting male make this a stand-out shot for me in the Animal Behaviour category.'

NEIL BYGRAVE <

Camouflaged Fallow Stags
(Fallow Deer, *Dama dama*)
Parkland Deer, Devon, England

During the October rut a number of the Fallow Stags (usually the more subordinate) will rake up as much vegetation as possible with their antlers and then parade proudly. As I photographed this behaviour I was lucky enough to align two stags back to back, which made for an impactful and interesting image.

GLYN THOMAS ∧

Puffin Fighting on Inner Farne
(Atlantic Puffin, *Fratercula arctica*)
Inner Farne, Farne Islands, Coast of Northumberland, England

I visit the Farnes most years to photograph the puffins. By the lighthouse on Inner Farne I was watching a group of puffins when suddenly one of them attacked another. They were fighting for around 10 seconds and this was my favourite image.

LEE MOTT

Grace
(Osprey, *Pandion haliaetus*)
Aviemore, Scotland

I set out over a period of two mornings to capture Ospreys seconds after
leaving the water and hopefully with fish. I wanted to capture some blurred
movement of the wings, but wanted to use enough shutter speed to freeze
the bird's head. I suddenly realised that the reflections on this still but dull
morning would play an important part in the image.

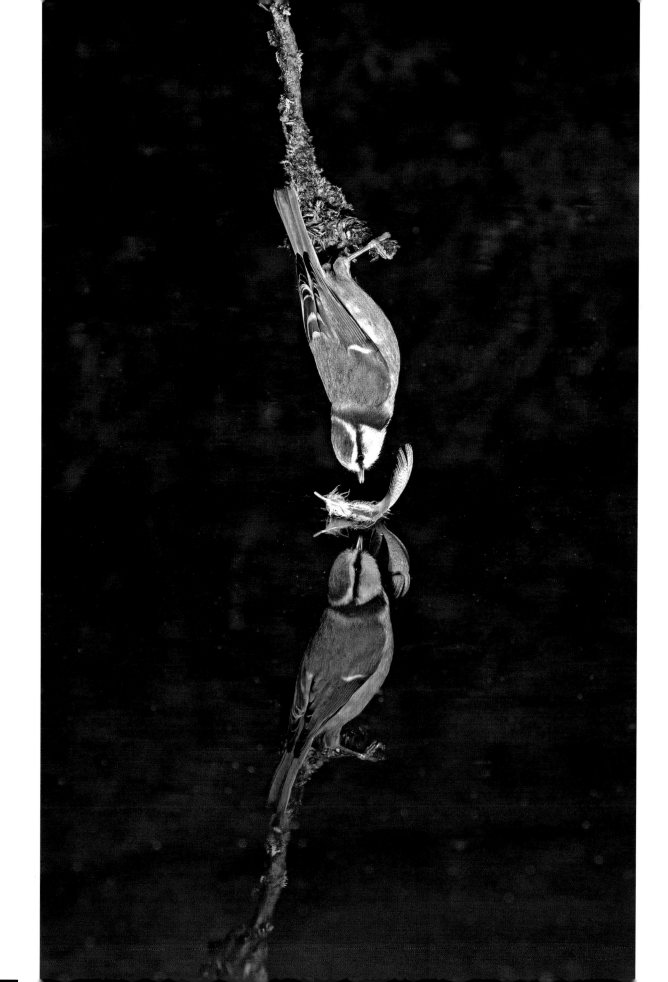

PHILIP KIRK >

Standing Room Only
(Herring gull, *Larus argentatus*)
Seahouses, Northumberland, England

I was having a snack in the car park at Seahouses when I noticed this unusual behaviour. It happened twice, as the gull on top flew off then came back, so I hastily grabbed my camera. I was lucky as it came back a third time and then they both flew off.

PAUL SAWER <

Blue Tit Taking Feather
(Blue Tit, *Parus caeruleus*)
Peasenhall, Suffolk, England

I spent two days making a pond and another day creating a hide. It took me a further day to perfect the lighting, for which I used three flashguns. Initially I was taking images of birds drinking from strategically placed perches and noticed a bird collect a feather from the edge of the pond. This inspired me to place a feather under the perch and after a couple of hours a Blue Tit collected it.

PETER WARNE

Great Spotted Woodpecker Exhausted by Winter Chill

(Great Spotted Woodpecker, *Dendrocopos major*)
Woodford Green, Essex, England

I live close to Epping Forest and can attract Great Spotted Woodpeckers into my garden with suitable food. The silver birch in the picture is false in the sense that it is a lopped tree which I erected by bolting it to a hardwood garden post strategically hidden from view. The birch is drilled with holes and filled each day with a mix of peanut butter, lard and breadcrumbs and I regularly attract three birds; two male, one female. For this image I photographed their visits through a thin glass window at the end of the house. At the end of last November the weather suddenly turned very cold and this bird flew in for food and then fell asleep. The white patches in the background are snow.

PETER WARNE

Avocets Bickering at Dawn on the Scrape at Blue-House Farm
(Avocet, *Recurvirostra avosetta*)
North Fambridge, Essex, England

Blue House Farm is a Site of Special Scientific Interest (SSSI), managed and developed by the Essex Wildlife Trust. I had reconnoitred the site on three occasions and watched the excited displays of the avocets as they fought for the prime nest sites on the scrape. I picked a fine morning in March and was set up in the hide at about 7am. At this hour they were close to the hide and I took many pictures of the birds and their reflections. At about 8am, the sun rose to an extent that sent a wash of orange light over the water. I was able to take about five pictures before the moment disappeared. Throughout, the birds continued to argue over territory and move pieces of weed, which were clearly important to them.

RANA DIAS <

Somersault. The Joy of a Bath in the Morning
(Mute Swan, *Cygnus olor*)
Earlswood Common, Earlswood, Surrey, England

It was a freezing early morning in January. I was at the lower lake in Earlswood Common, capturing swans taking off under the beautiful morning light. I'm a regular visitor to this place but have never captured such an abstract display. She was performing shallow dives many times and this shot was a bonus. The lighting and timing was perfect and I ended up taking almost 40 shots!

THOMAS HANAHOE Λ

Marsh Harrier with a Stick
(Marsh Harrier, *Circus aeruginosus*)
Fowlmere, Cambridgeshire, England

I have photographed this male bird for the last few years. He usually appears at the RSPB Fowlmere Reserve in early April and prepares a nest platform for the female who arrives a couple of weeks later. With the lens resting on the window, the photograph was taken from an elevated hide whilst the bird was collecting nesting material.

CRAIG CHURCHILL

Hanging Around
(Nuthatch, *Sitta europaea*)
Hampton, Worcestershire, England

A friend of mine has a drinking pool set up to photograph woodland species and had kindly invited me down to photograph the Nuthatch that was visiting the pool that day. A perch was put in place and it was then a case of waiting until the Nuthatch perched in the right place and hung over the pool to retrieve fallen nuts.

ANDREW PARKINSON

Dunlin Tug-of-War
(Dunlin, *Calidris alpina*)
Shetland Islands, Scotland

Dressed in a dry suit I spent the day lying in a large rock pool
photographing waders feeding on a remote Scottish beach. With so many
birds to point my lens at, the difficulty was trying to be focused on the right
bird at the right time. On this occasion I got lucky as this Dunlin started
pulling out a worm just as I focused on it.

DES ONG

Love Bites
(Common Lizard, *Lacerta vivipara*)
Abergavenny, Monmouthshire, Wales

At first it looked as if there was going to be a fight, with one of the lizards trying to bite the other. It became apparent later that this aggressor was in fact the male. It worked its grip from just below the hind legs to just above them, before coiling its tail around the female and mating. Both subjects were temporarily contained while this image was taken, and released to the exact original location immediately after.

THOMAS HANAHOE

White-tailed Sea Eagle with a Fish
(White-tailed Sea Eagle, *Haliaeetus albicilla*)
Isle of Skye, Scotland

The photograph was taken at about 7.30am from a boat out of Portree
harbour. The Sea Eagle was hunting and come close to the boat to take
fish. The sea was relatively choppy causing the boat to move up and down.
In order to keep focused on the bird, I rested my shoulder against the
wheelhouse to steady the camera and lens while I took the shot.

URBAN
WILDLIFE

URBAN WILDLIFE WINNER

DAVID BIGGS

Champagne Starling
(European Starling, *Sturnes Vulgaris*)
Bayston Hill, Shrewsbury, Shropshire, England

A roost of starlings flew into a group of trees behind my house. I quickly grabbed my camera, stood on top of the garden furniture and started to photograph these wonderful creatures. The birds finally settled and then there was silence until something spooked them and the tree burst into life. As they left I shed a tear. This was nature at its best, wild and untamed.

DOUG MACKENZIE DODDS <
HIGHLY COMMENDED

Tabby Cat with Blackbird Nestling
(Blackbird, *Turdus merula*)
Reading, Berkshire, England

A contentious subject I know – of a domestic tom tabby cat raiding a blackbird's nest in a town-house garden. I didn't know whether to even take this shot, but I think I'm glad I did. I didn't relish the photographic subject of course, but love it or hate it, I hoped the eventual image itself would have a certain power to it.

DAMIAN WATERS >   HIGHLY COMMENDED

Flower Power
(Brown Hare, *Lepus capensis*)
Wirral, Merseyside, England

I have been photographing Brown Hares for many years and usually strive to take images of them in a natural setting. On this occasion, by pure chance, I came across one enjoying a free handout of food in a local cemetery.

MATT SMITH   HIGHLY COMMENDED

Gulls Fighting in London
(Black Headed Gull, *Chroicocephalus ridibundus*)
Westminster Bridge, London, England

I had brought some seeds to attract pigeons, but since the gulls had taken over the area I changed tactics and borrowed a piece of bread from a tourist. I sat there for an hour, breaking off small chunks until I had these two fighting over one. Usually I like to plan shots, but in this instance, I feel I was lucky to get it.

TERRY WHITTAKER/2020VISION   HIGHLY COMMENDED

Winter Heron
(Grey Heron, *Ardea cinerea*)
Reddish Vale Country Park, Greater Manchester, England

Visitors to the country park on the outskirts of Manchester feed the herons with fish scraps or sprats bought from the local supermarket. During a period of cold, dark weather last winter I spent several days photographing them. I placed a remotely triggered camera and flashes by pools on the ice where the birds would be reflected. I got a lucky break when the sun briefly broke through the grey.

PAUL HOBSON

A Hedgehog at Church
(Hedgehog, *Erinaceus europaeus*)
Sheffield, South Yorkshire, England

I have been working with a hedgehog rescue centre for three years. Many of the hogs are released back into suitable habitat in Sheffield and I often follow up on them over the next few weeks. This is a released hog that stayed around a local church for a few weeks. I wanted to show the connection with the church and its nocturnal habits. I used a small flash with a tube to reduce the beam to fall subtly on the hog.

MICK HOULT

Kestrel on Windowsill Sheltering from Rain
(Kestrel, *Falco tinnunculus*)
Glossop, Derbyshire, England

This bird had used the windowsill of my attic workroom as a perch several times and on this occasion had been caught in a heavy downpour. It was resting with at least the window-side eye closed, so I was able to sneak past to fetch a camera and creep back to grab this single shot before it flew.

BEN HALL

Peregrine Perched on Hotel Roof
(Peregrine Falcon, *Falco peregrinus*)
Manchester, England

I recently undertook a commission to photograph a pair of Peregrines that were nesting in Manchester city centre. I gained permission to shoot from a nearby hotel rooftop and spent many hours observing the nest. One afternoon, one of the parent birds landed on the corner of the roof I was on. With adrenaline flowing, I managed to creep along the roofline and emerged less than 10 feet from the bird. It peered straight into the lens for several seconds whilst I fired a succession of shots, capturing the intensity of its stare.

JAMES SMITH

After the Storm
(Common Starfish, *Asterias rubens*)
Blackpool, Lancashire, England

After strong winds in the area overnight, thousands of starfish appeared on Blackpool beach. It's a species not usually associated with urban wildlife, and you wouldn't think that above the pier is one of Blackpool's most famous ferris wheels.

KEVIN GUTTRIDGE

Black-headed Gull on Warehouse Roof
(Black-headed Gull, *Larus ridibundus*)
Rochester, Kent, England

This picture was taken while I was at work. I work next
to a river and when it's high tide, I noticed that the gulls
roosted on the roof, waiting for the tide to go back out.
I climbed on top of a stack of wood and was lying on
my back to take the photograph.

ANDY ROUSE

Little Owl on Barn
(Little Owl, *Athene noctua*)
Wiltshire, England

As part of my Little Owl project last summer I worked at several nest locations. This one was in a barn setting and every night the owls perched on a barn roof before flying into the next box.

PAUL HOBSON

Wood Mouse Running on a Shelf in My Garden Shed
(Wood Mouse, *Apodemus sylvaticus*)
Sheffield, South Yorkshire, England

Wood mice live in my shed in my garden in Sheffield and regularly raid the bird food stored there. I often see them running on the shelves. The image is taken at night in winter through the window from the outside as a mouse investigates a shelf by the window. Inside, the shed is lit by candles which create the yellow highlight effect.

JAMES SMITH

The Congregation
(European Starling, *Sturnus vulgaris*)
Blackpool, Lancashire, England

Up to one hundred thousand starlings congregate in Blackpool over the winter months. They flock for protection against predatory birds such as peregrines and sparrowhawks; as you can see in this image it's hard to distinguish just one bird from the flock. I photographed starlings for five months for a university project and found it incredible how many people overlook this unique spectacle that is happening right before them. Hopefully this image may change that.

HIDDEN
BRITAIN

SPONSORED BY

BUGLIFE

LESLIE HOLBURN

Scorpion Fly on a Leaf
(Scorpion Fly, *Panorpa communis*)
Ebchester, County Durham, England

I have a small pond in the garden for wildlife. When watching for Dragonfly and Damselfly I noticed the Scorpion Fly, so on went the wellies and in I went. Even though the light was poor I still managed to get this shot.

Three Small Skippers on Foxglove Seedheads
(Small Skipper Butterflies, *Thymelicus sylvestris*)
Pamber Forest Nature Reserve,
Tadley, Hampshire, England

The day had started off bright and sunny but began
to cloud over in the afternoon. I was walking through
Pamber Forest, near Tadley in Hampshire, when I came
across these butterflies settled down at the edge of the
ride. I got this image using natural backlighting to show
off the hairs on both the insects and plant just before
the sun re-emerged, stirring the insects back into life
and they flew off.

JOHN H. BRACKENBURY   HIGHLY COMMENDED

Four-spotted Orbweaver
(Four-spotted Orbweaver, *Araneus quadratus*)
Mare's Way, Cambridgeshire, England

Large females are common in early autumn, having spent the summer
months feeding. This shot was taken from ground level, looking directly up
at the subject framed against the sky.

WILLIAM RICHARDSON   HIGHLY COMMENDED

Ladybird on Rose
(Harlequin Ladybird, *Harmonia axyridis*)
London, England

In the early morning after a brief shower of rain I was taking photographs of roses in the rose garden. I took a picture of this ladybird on a perfect rose, bathed in raindrops.

ALEX WINSER ∧   HIGHLY COMMENDED

Adonis Blues Basking in the Morning Sunshine
(Adonis Blues, *Polyommatus bellargus*)
Denbies Hillside, Dorking, Surrey, England

Backlit by the sunrise, these Adonis Blues were drying off from a night in the long grass, ready for their maiden flight of the day. A 4am start was required to ensure I was able to locate my subjects and set up before sunrise. I used a shallow depth of field to throw the background out of focus and highlight the primary butterfly. I just love these dawn shoots, especially when I get results like this.

ROSS HODDINOTT >   HIGHLY COMMENDED

Backlit Blue-tailed Damselfly Portrait
(Blue-tailed Damselfly, *Ischnura elegans*)
Tamar Lakes, Cornwall, England

Damselflies are one of my favourite subjects. During summer, I regularly visit local lakes and ponds in order to find and photograph these colourful insects. In the evenings, they will rest up for the night on grasses near the water's edge. I noticed this male Blue-tailed Damselfly backlit by the evening sun. Its background was in shade, helping the insect's large, disproportionate eyes to really stand out.

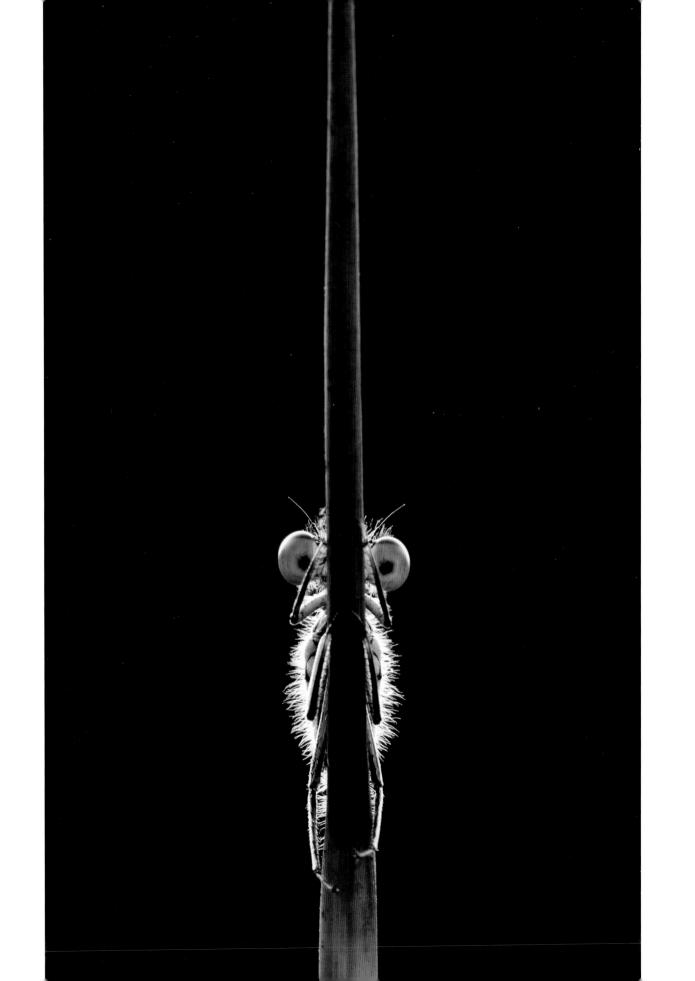

PHIL McLEAN <   HIGHLY COMMENDED

Orange-Tip on Water Avens
(Orange-Tip Butterfly, *Anthocharis cardamines*)
Chirnside, Berwickshire, Scottish Borders

I had observed these butterflies flying during the day along the banks of the
River Whiteadder, near my home in Berwickshire. I returned in the evening
when they were less active, found this one and photographed it on water
avens. I used natural backlighting to show off the fine hairs on both the
butterfly and the plant.

PAUL HOBSON ∧

Bankside Orbweaver Amongst Fruiting Moss
(Bankside Orbweaver, *Larinioides cornutus*)
Sheffield, South Yorkshire, England

I was walking through a local nature reserve in Sheffield, looking for
spiders, when I noticed a web between two bullrush heads that had started
to release seeds. On closer investigation I noticed this Orb Spider hiding
among the fluff of the seed heads. It was well camouflaged.

JAMIE CRAGGS

City Cricket (Katydid on my London balcony)
(Oak Bush-cricket, *Meconema thalassinum*)
East Finchley, London, England

One warm evening during summer this amazing
Katydid flew onto my second floor balcony in north
London. I used my old manual flash to backlight it in
order to highlight the long antennae against a black
background.

ROSS HODDINOTT/2020VISION

Banded Demoiselle
(Banded Demoiselle, *Calopteryx splendens*)
Tamar Lakes, Cornwall, England

After fine, still nights in spring and summer, insects can be found dew-covered and sparkling like jewels in the early morning light. If the forecast looks promising, I set my alarm for sunrise and visit local wildlife reserves in search. On this occasion, I discovered this male Banded Demoiselle glistening among the reeds. An area of shadow behind the insect created a simple black backdrop.

DAVE PRESSLAND

Speckled Bush-cricket nymph
(Speckled Bush-cricket nymph, *Leptophyes punctatissima*)
Belvedere, Kent, England

Nipping out to top up the bird feeders one morning, still in my dressing gown, I spotted these cricket nymphs. I realised they were perfectly positioned to get an out-of-focus red peony bloom behind them for a very striking image. I used three lens-mounted flashes to light the insect and a fourth flash on a bracket extending past the cricket to light the peony. I was late for work but it was worth it.

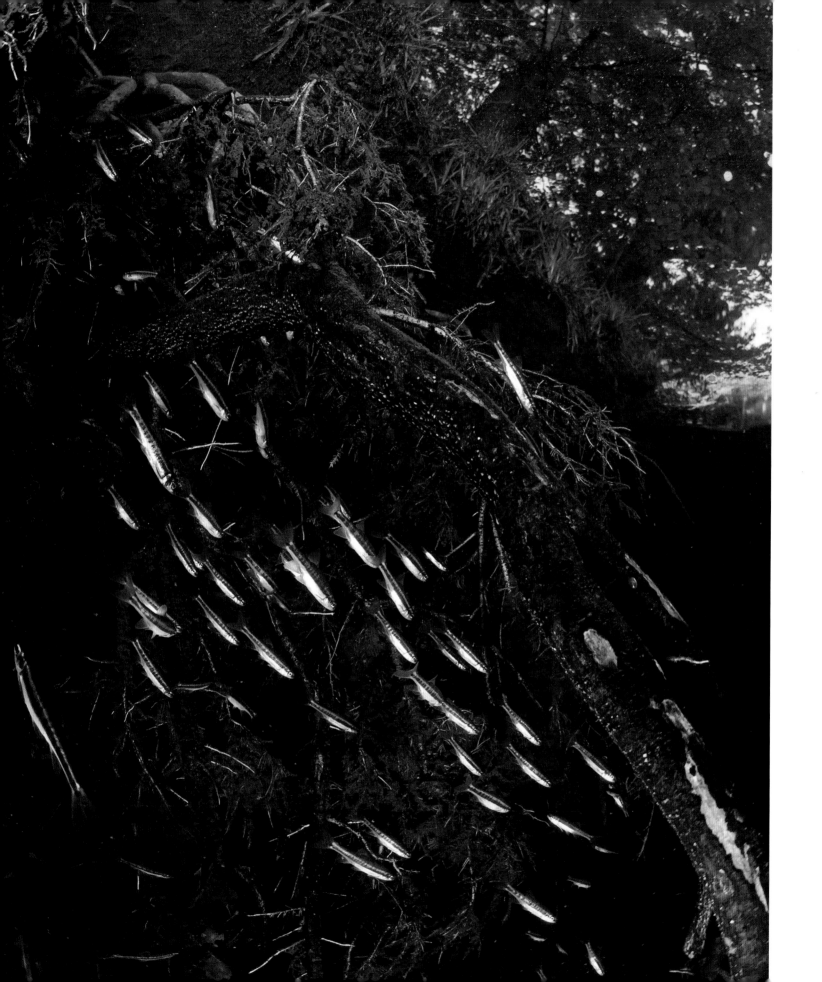

DAN BOLT <

Minnow in the River Dart
(Minnow, *Phoxinus phoxinus*)
River Dart, Ashburton, Dartmoor, Devon, England

Over a two-week period I spend a total of 10 hours
in the river with this group of fish, slowly gaining
their trust. Due to their skittish nature I was limited to
snorkelling and breath-holding to the river bed in order
to shoot upwards through the tree roots in which they
take shelter. The bubbles from scuba gear would have
made this shot impossible.

MARK WEBSTER >

Nudibranch Feeding on Hydrozoans Growing on Kelp Frond
(Nudibranch or Sea Slug, *Eubranchus farrani*)
Pendennis Point Reef, Falmouth Bay, Cornwall, England

In early spring Nudibranchs begin to appear in
sheltered shallow water to breed and feed. This pretty
species is very small, perhaps 10mm, and so I used a
macro lens and a dioptre to increase magnification.
I watched this nudibranch for perhaps 30 minutes,
waiting for it to move slowly into position in the curve
formed by the kelp frond it was feeding on.

MALCOLM SCHUYL

Marmalade Hoverfly Feeding on Poppy Flower
(Marmalade Hoverfly, *Episyrphus balteatus*)
Ewelme, Oxfordshire, England

I noticed that the hoverflies were attracted to the poppy
flowers that were out in the garden. I particularly liked
the combination of colours. I set up a camera on a
tripod and waited until one rested in a good position,
and took the picture using a little flash lighting.

114

RACHEL SCOPES

Poised on a Petal
(Two-spot Ladybird, *Adalia bipunctata*)
Horncastle, Lincolnshire, England

A wet summer's day can be frustrating, but once the showers have passed and gentle evening sunlight breaks through, I love to escape outside. Lying down on a wet lawn can reveal hidden beauties such as this ladybird poised on a petal of a raindrop-adorned daisy.

DES ONG

Chrysalis of a Peacock
(Peacock Butterfly, *Inachis io*)
Loughborough, Leicestershire, England

This striking chrysalis belongs to an equally colourful Peacock Butterfly. At the time, I had no idea what pupa this was. What grabbed my attention was the alien-like shape and the bright colours. To overcome the bright conditions, I shot it against the shaded part of a tree, rendering the background black. The blade of grass above acted as a natural diffuser, softening the light. A small reflector was used to lift the shadow areas.

DANNY BEATH

Mayfly in Silhouette
(Green Drake, *Ephemera danica*)
Shrewsbury, Shropshire, England

There were millions of these Common Mayflies swarming along the river in the middle of Shrewsbury, painting the sky black with huge clouds on a sultry June evening. I waited until the sky blushed pink at sunset before I located a nicely silhouetted specimen to photograph against the sky.

COAST AND MARINE

SPONSORED BY

WWF

COAST AND OVERALL WINNER

RICHARD SHUCKSMITH

Jellyfish in the Blue Sea of Sula Sgeir
(Jellyfish, *Pelegia noctiluca*)
Off Sula Sgeir, Scotland
See page 23

MARCEL VAN BALKOM HIGHLY COMMENDED

Diving Gannet Near the Bass
(Gannet, *Morus bassanus or Sula bassana*)
Bass Rock, Scotland

We left in the early morning by boat towards the Bass. The day started in a dense fog. During the trip I feared bad conditions and a change of very difficult circumstances. Every now and then there was a Gannet flying by but it was difficult to shoot the desired pictures. Almost when we reached the Bass the mist was clearing and there was beautiful light, which allowed me to make this picture of the diving Gannet.

Grey Seal Beneath Cliffs
(Grey Seal, *Halichoerus grypus*)
Lundy Island, Devon, England

To produce this image I designed a super-sized front element for my underwater camera, which measures 55cm across. This allows me to shoot both above and below the surface at the same time in rough British seas. After much waiting in the cold water this young seal came close enough for the shot.

ANDREW PARKINSON   HIGHLY COMMENDED

Gannet in Flight
(Gannet, *Morus bassanus*)
Shetland Islands, Scotland

In biting northerly Force Eight winds I sat huddled at the top of precipitous cliffs trying to encourage my freezing hands to function properly. As I was buffeted about like a rag doll I tried to build compositions from the raging seas below. Here I like the way the breaking waves gives a sense of speed and grace to the formidable Gannet.

JANE MORGAN   HIGHLY COMMENDED

The Eye of a Tope
(Tope, *Galeorhinus galeus*)
Bawden Rock, Cornwall, England

My buddy was busy collecting seaweed samples
for the Cornwall Wildlife Trust when we stumbled upon
a tope (shark) resting on the reef. At around 1.5 metres
in length my macro lens couldn't record the entire
animal so I opted to try and take a close-up photo of its
eye. Due to the position of the animal it was difficult to
get a good angle with my camera but the shark seemed
completely relaxed.

KRIS WORSLEY   HIGHLY COMMENDED

Sun Terns
(Arctic Tern, *Sterna paradisaea*)
Farne Islands, Northumbria, England

I spent three days on the Farne Islands photographing sea birds. On this day I found the harsh midday sun difficult to work with, so I decided to make it a part of the image. I particularly liked the pattern created when two birds fluttered in front of me, but in this picture a third tern just happened to fly across the sun with its beak open. Sometimes a bit of good luck doesn't hurt.

JAMIE CRAGGS

Moon Jellyfish

(Moon Jellyfish, *Aurelia aurita*)
London Aquarium, London, England

Jellyfish in captivity make amazing displays in public aquariums.
I photographed jellyfish which had been cultured in captivity for display at
the London Aquarium. Their stomachs are full of orange plankton, which
sets off the jellyfish well against the dark blue background.

MATTHEW OXLEY

The Nest Builder
(Corkwing Wrasse, *Symphodus melops*)
Falmouth, Cornwall, England

I came across this Corkwing Wrasse off the coast of Falmouth in Cornwall. He was aggressively defending his nest from what he perceived to be danger. Once he became comfortable with my presence he began tending the nest, bringing debris, seaweed and other vegetation to keep the eggs safe. He will defend his nest in this manner until the eggs hatch.

JANE MORGAN

Sea Anemones
(Sea Anemone, *Sagartia elegans*)
Paul's Rock, Scilly Islands, England

I was photographing Jewel Anemones on Paul's Rock in the Scilly Islands when I came across this colony of beautiful *Sagartia elegans*. A mixture of individuals with pink and white tentacles covered a large area. They were just as pretty as the jewels.

JANE MORGAN

Jewel Anemones
(Jewel Anemone, *Corynactis viridis*)
Paul's Rock, Scilly Islands, England

I was trying to get a different angle on one of the nation's favourite
anemones by dropping below the reef and shooting up to get
a negative background.

ALEX TATTERSALL

Dobbin
(Spiny Seahorse, *Hippocampus hystrix*)
Dorset, England

Whilst out on a dive we came across this beautiful specimen of a Spiny
Seahorse. Taken under the licence of Dr Alex Mustard.

ROBERT BAILEY

Grey Seal Behaviour
(Grey Seal, *Halichoerus grypus*)
Farne Islands, England

We embarked on a weekend trip with the East Midlands Underwater Photography Group (EMUP) and spent two days diving and photographing grey seals last October. Perfect conditions afforded us many opportunities to capture interesting behaviour. I was lucky enough to be in the right place to capture these seals engaged in what appears to be courting behaviour.

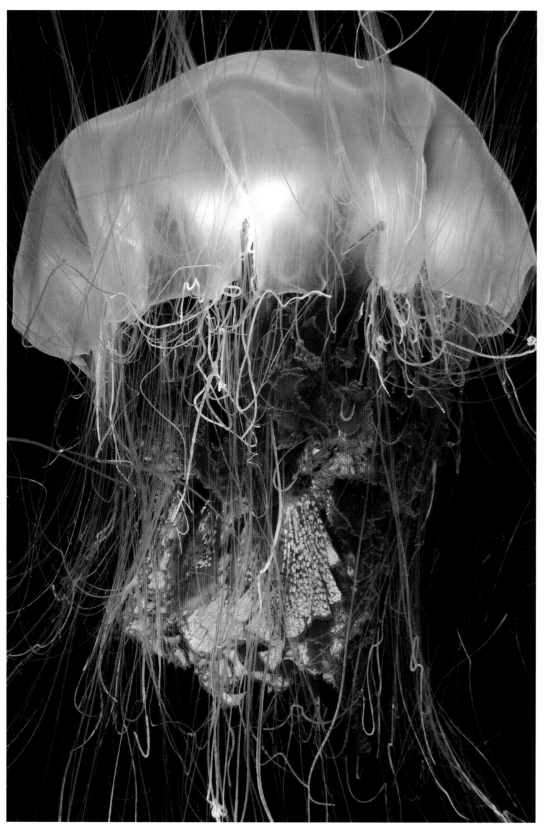

ELAINE WHITEFORD <

Lion's Mane Jellyfish in Loch Fyne
(Lion's Mane Jellyfish, *Cyanea capillata*)
Loch Fyne, Argyll, Scotland

I came across this Lion's Mane Jellyfish drifting along at a depth of around 10 metres in Loch Fyne. In mid-water there was nothing for the light of my strobe to bounce off, so I had to get very close to the Lion's Mane to ensure effective lighting. Hovering alongside such a magnificent creature and admiring it full-frame in my lens was a real privilege.

MARK WEBSTER >

Compass Jellyfish
(Compass Jellyfish, *Chrysaora hysoscella*)
Pendennis Point Reef, Falmouth Bay, Cornwall, England

There are normally two plankton blooms in Cornwall: one in May/June and one in July/August. The second occurs when the surface temperature has risen to perhaps 14 degrees, which also increases the prospect of seeing jellyfish in large numbers. The pattern on a Compass Jellyfish resembles the cardinal points on a traditional ship's compass and can often be seen in swarms of hundreds of individuals.

ROBERT BAILEY

Grey Seal Behaviour
(Grey Seal, *Halichoerus grypus*)
Farne Islands, England

We embarked on a weekend trip with the East Midlands Underwater
Photography Group (EMUP) and spent two days diving and photographing
grey seals last October. Perfect conditions afforded us many opportunities
to capture interesting behaviour. This female approached and was very
curious about me, not at all aggressive.

DANNY BEATH

Spawning Starfish
(Common Starfish, *Asterius rubens*)
Near Barmouth, West Wales

I found thousands of these starfish in pools at high water mark following a spring tide, after they had been spawning in the shallows. They were being picked off by gulls in many places but most survived to return to the sea on the next high tide.

RICHARD SHUCKSMITH

Grey Seal Haul Out
(Grey Seal, *Halichoerus grypus*)
Off the west coast of Scotland

There were over 400 Grey Seals using this beach on a remote island on the
west coast of Scotland. I was camping there to photograph the island and its
wildlife when I got stranded due to the bad weather. Strong winds battered
the coastline and at night, above the noise of the wind, the seals howled
and called to each other causing eerie sounds to cross the island. I spent
most of my time crawling around the camp keeping a very low profile as any
movement directed towards the beach would have the seals into the water.

LEE MOTT

Winter Calm
(Iceland Gull, *Larus glaucoides*)
Lerwick, Shetland, Scotland

Iceland Gulls are scarce winter visitors to the UK. A few are annual visitors to Shetland and particularly Lerwick Harbour. On a rare winter day in Shetland with no wind I headed out, hopeful of some nice reflections. The birds skipped along the surface, picking up tiny particles of food. I had just a couple of hours of magical light before the clouds rolled in and it began to snow.

ALEXANDER MUSTARD/2020VISION

Spider Crab Aggregation
(Spider Crab, *Maja squinado*)
Burton Bradstock, Dorset, England

After much research and advice from scientists at the National Oceanography Centre, Southampton, I finally had a time and place to search for this amazing aggregation of Spider Crabs close to the popular tourist beach at Burton Bradstock. The aggregation seems more to do with moulting, and while some mating takes place, many of the crabs are not yet mature.

ANDREW PARKINSON

Gannets in a Force Eight
(Gannet, *Morus bassanus*)
Shetland Islands, Scotland

With this image I wanted to show the gannets as a part of their dramatic coastal environment but I also wanted to try and make the image look like a painting. In order to do this I stopped right down to F16 to bring the whole scene into sharp focus and then it was a matter of waiting for the image to reveal itself.

THOMAS HANAHOE

Gannets Fishing
(Gannet, *Sula bassana*)
Bass Rock, Scotland

The picture was taken from a boat travelling from Dunbar harbour to the Bass Rock. The Gannets were diving for fish thrown into the water by the boatman, which caused a feeding frenzy. The boat rolled with the waves and the challenge was to photograph the birds just before they entered the water as they dived for the fish.

CHRISTINE ROBERTS

Jewel Anemones
(Jewel Anemone, *Corynactis viridis*)
Raglan Reef, Manacles, Cornwall, England

Raglan Reef rises from a depth of 45 metres to within seven metres of the surface. This photograph was taken at 20 metres and with little ambient light available at this depth, strobes were essential to highlight the colouration. Jewel anemones form dense clusters in areas with strong tidal movement, covering the rock faces with exotic colour. Fortunately, a neap tide allowed me more time to focus.

WILDLIFE IN MY BACKYARD

SPONSORED BY

COUNTRYSIDE COUNCIL

FOR WALES

RANA DIAS

Busy Wasp on Blackberries
(Common Wasp, *Vespula vulgaris*)
Horley, Surrey, England

This greedy wasp never wanted to leave the blackberry hedge in our backyard. He wasn't interested in what I was doing and was having a fabulous time munching on the berries. The lighting was just right and he gave me the best pose.

RON COULTER   HIGHLY COMMENDED

Jay Taking Off
(Jay, *Garrulus glandarius*)
Buckinghamshire, England

I set up a log in my back garden in continuous snow, put out some peanuts and just waited for four hours in a hide. The temperature was below freezing point.

THOMAS HANAHOE   HIGHLY COMMENDED

Squirrel with a Conker
(Grey Squirrel, *Sciurus carolinensis*)
Potton, Bedfordshire, England

Conkers were placed in a small container so that to reach them the squirrel had to jump from a farm gate and then back to the gate with his prize. The camera was set up close to the stash of conkers and fired by remote control as the squirrel escaped with the conker in his mouth.

CHARLES EVERITT   HIGHLY COMMENDED

Sanctuary
(Bullfinch, *Pyrrhula pyrrhula*)
Edinburgh, Midlothian, Scotland

This male Bullfinch was a regular visitor to the crabapple tree in my garden, which serves as a bustling hub for birds passing to and from the feeders. The tree was exceptionally busy during the cold winter with blackbirds feeding frenetically on the crabapples. When the snow came, I was able to photograph some of the birds in the tree and amongst the apples from a bedroom window.

CHRIS GRABSKI   HIGHLY COMMENDED

Very Hungry Dragonfly in Kent
(Southern Hawker, *Aeshna cyanea*)
Frindsbury, Kent, England

I was about to go shopping with my family. Before
getting in the car, I noticed two dragonflies in the
garden and I could not resist taking a few photographs.
I am very pleased with the outcome.

ALBEL SINGH <

Bee(ing) Cross Pollination
(*Garden Bumblebee, Phlomis fruiticosa*)
Birmingham, West Midlands, England

Pollination makes the world go round. To my
amazement it can be quite sophisticated. You cannot
see the anthers and stigma until the bee goes into the
flower. The anthers and stigma rub against the body of
the bee, the pollen sticks to the back of the bee, and as
the bee visits other flowers, the stigma receives a mix of
pollen, thus accomplishing cross pollination.

MARK HAMBLIN >

Robin Perched on Spade Handle in Snow
(Robin, *Erithacus rubecula*)
Carrbridge, Inverness-shire, Scotland

The hard winter weather that enveloped Scotland
during late November 2010 brought difficult times
for local birds. For more than two weeks, up to four
robins were visiting the feeding area in the garden.
They would line up in anticipation as I approached,
one even landing on my hand to take scraps of food.
Sitting quietly without a hide I enjoyed several days
photographing them at close quarters.

MARK HAMBLIN

Goldfinch Perched on Crab Apples in Snow
(Goldfinch, *Carduelis carduelis*)
Carrbridge, Inverness-shire, Scotland

Goldfinches have been visiting my garden for the past three or four years with a particular fondness for nyger seeds. My quest this year was to capture them in the snow and so I set up a sprig of crab apple close to a feeder and entered my hide early one morning after a heavy fall of snow. The early morning winter sun perfectly highlighted the bird's colourful plumage but quickly put pay to the snow, which soon melted from the perch.

HABITAT

SPONSORED BY
COUNTRYSIDE JOBS SERVICE

HABITAT WINNER

HABITAT WINNER

IAN PAUL HASKELL

Hare in Morning Light with Hoar Frost
(Brown Hare, *Lepus europaeus*)
Norfolk

A morning spent in a hoar frost with beautiful morning light. The hare was running towards me through a lovely avenue of trees. The light was spectacular and enhanced by the frost.

BEN HALL   HIGHLY COMMENDED

Red Grouse Perched on Gritstone Boulder

(Red Grouse, *Lagopus lagopus*)
Peak District, England

During the summer I was working on Moorland birds for a commission and made frequent visits to an area of the Dark Peak that was home to a family of Red Grouse. I had pictured this image in my mind but had to return on numerous occasions before the grouse finally perched on the edge of the valley. I used a wide-angle lens so as to include a backdrop of rolling Peak landscape and a distant reservoir.

BEN HALL   HIGHLY COMMENDED

Dipper Perched on Moss-covered Waterfall
(Dipper, *Cinclus cinclus*)
Peak District, England

I had been observing a family of Dippers nesting behind a waterfall for several weeks. By setting up a tripod and using a slow shutter speed I was able to capture the movement of the water whilst keeping the bird sharp. I took a sequence of images, in only one of which the bird had remained still throughout the exposure.

ALEXANDER MUSTARD/2020VISION
HIGHLY COMMENDED

Toad in the Hole
(Common Toad, *Bufo bufo*)
River Orchy, Highlands, Scotland

On assignment for 2020VISION I was searching the River Orchy for life, hoping for frogs and toads. The first pair of toads I found were at the bottom of the river, 20 feet below the surface. This individual was swimming on the surface – I photographed it in silhouette against the sky and trees. I like the monochrome look of the image and how the trees are still, showing it is early spring when the toads are mating.

JUDGE'S CHOICE: STEVE YOUNG, *BWPA WILDLIFE PHOTOGRAPHER OF THE YEAR 2010*

"…imaginative and original image that powerfully portrays the importance of the environment and ecosystems that sustain the wildlife within them"

So said the guidelines for would-be entrants to the Habitat section and I can think of no better example of those guidelines than this shot of a swimming frog taken from a unique and original angle by Alex Mustard. My first thought on seeing this image was, 'how was that taken?' A bit of luck, a lot of patience, plus knowledge and skill must have all played their part, but it is a truly memorable image and one of my favourites from this year's competition.'

Wood Mouse
(Wood Mouse, *Apodemus sylvaticus*)
Llyn Elsi, above Betws-y-Coed, Snowdonia National Park, North Wales

Having just finished a quiet picnic in this lovely part of Snowdonia National Park, I realised that I had company. A Wood Mouse was feeding only an arm's length away. I very slowly attached a wide-angle lens so I could include the surrounding habitat, quietly rolled onto my belly and I was eye-level with this beautiful creature. She wasn't at all disturbed by me and I savoured this encounter for perhaps five minutes or so until she scampered away.

MARK HAMBLIN   HIGHLY COMMENDED

Puffin on Hermaness Cliffs
(Atlantic Puffin, *Fratercula arctica*)
Hermaness, Unst, Shetland, Scotland

The puffins on Hermaness cliffs are used to seeing visiting humans that take
the long walk along some of the most spectacular cliffs in the UK. During
my visit to Shetland last summer I made four or five visits to the cliffs,
mainly for the gannets. But on one evening about a dozen puffins were
loafing around and allowed me to approach very closely using a wide-angle
lens to include the background as part of the picture.

BEN HALL   HIGHLY COMMENDED

Fallow Deer Peering through Ferns
(Fallow deer, *Dama dama*)
Cheshire, England

For this image my aim was to show the deer in the context of its woodland habitat. I chose to shoot from a distance and frame the deer amongst the surrounding trees. By keeping myself low I was able to blur the ferns in the foreground to add depth.

MARK N THOMAS <

Diamonds in the Deep
(Diamond Sturgeon, *Acipenser gueldenstaedtii*)
Jackdaw Quarry, Over Kellet, Lancashire, England

On a cold March morning I watched as the sturgeon meandered over the quarry floor, using its barbells to search for food amongst the weed and silt. I waited in the cold water, five degrees centigrade, until the fish passed within inches before taking the photo.

CHRIS O'REILLY ∧

Capercaillie
(Capercaillie, *Tetrao urugallus*)
Loughborough, Leicestershire, England

The phenomena of the 'rogue' male capercaillie occurs infrequently, but when an instance does arise the bird will defend his territory against all-comers – including humans. This rogue male had no hesitation in confronting me as I visited his territory well in advance of the breeding season. While I secured a handful of images depicting the classic territorial display – upright stance, fanned-tail, head thrown back and furious calling – I was uncomfortable that the bird was wasting energy on me for the sake of a few pictures.

167

ELLIOTT NEEP

Red Deer Stag at Rest in Highland Habitat
(Red Deer, *Cervus elaphus*)
Near Glengarry, Highlands, Scotland

As I rounded a Highland track, I saw the stag just resting on the verge. At
first it stood up and walked away, then came to rest in the moorland grass.
Getting out of the car would have sent the stag running, so I edged the car
forward and hoped for the best. The stag was relaxed and I managed to line
up the stag with Loch Quoich and the Highland scenery. Using a wide-angle
lens, I wanted to capture the iconic scene, but the light was strong.
I exposed the image as brightly as I could to preserve highlight details.

GREG MORGAN

Marsh Harrier at Dusk

(Marsh Harrier, *Circus aeruginosus*)
Elmley Marshes RSPB Reserve, Isle of Sheppey, Kent, England

Although Marsh Harriers are rare birds of prey in the UK, the Isle of Sheppey is a great place to see them. I took this shot from the hide as the female came in to roost for the evening, with the last rays of the sun illuminating her feathers and the tops of the reeds.

DES ONG

The Secret World of Badger
(Badger, *Meles meles*)
Loughborough, Leicestershire, England

This was the result of a two-month long project to photograph badgers in daylight. This sett was fairly old and very extensive. By the time I finished, I had managed to attain a number of different images including some close-ups. But my favourite was this one, where I used a short focal length to provide a vista of the woodland through the canopies, giving a real sense of peeping into their secret world.

GRAHAM STOKES

Grey Squirrel in Log
(Grey Squirrel, *Sciurus carolinensis*)
Cornwall, England

While I was photographing a badger I had seen this inquisitive squirrel waiting to get some of the food I had left out for the badger. I hadn't seen a close-up photograph of a squirrel before and decided to try get a close-up shot of him inside a hollowed-out tree trunk.

BRITISH
SEASONS

SPONSORED BY

RSPB

ROSS HODDINOTT

SUMMER INSECTS
1. Thick-legged Flower Beetle on Corn Marigold
(Thick-legged Flower Beetle, *Oedemera nobilis*)
Pentire Point, near Newquay, Cornwall, England

I found this Thick-legged Flower Beetle feeding on a
corn marigold – the insect wasn't placed on the flower.
I adopted an overhead angle and, using a macro lens,
I filled the frame with the flower to maximise impact.

2. Backlit Marbled White Butterfly
(Marbled White Butterfly, *Melanargia galethea*)
Dunsdon Nature Reserve, Devon, England

Despite their name and appearance, Marbled White
Butterflies are actually members of the 'brown'
family. I photographed this insect early one morning.
Backlighting highlighted the markings and translucency
of its wings.

3. Backlit Banded Demoiselle
(Banded Demoiselle, *Calopteryx splenens*)
Tamar Lakes, Cornwall, England

I discovered this Banded Demoiselle early one fine
morning, just as the sun appeared above the horizon.
I intentionally shot in the light's direction, including
the sun in the top right corner to create a contrasty,
atmospheric image. The warm lighting epitomises
the season.

4. Newly Emerged Darter
(Common Darter, *Sympetrum striolatum*)
Tamar Lakes, Cornwall, England

This image was taken at my parent's pond one July
morning. The Common Darter Dragonfly was newly
emerged and drying in the sunshine. When you
look at the size and beauty of the insect it's hard to
comprehend that – until a few hours beforehand –
it had been a dark, ugly aquatic nymph.

1

JUDGE'S CHOICE: PAUL MITCHELL, *AA PUBLISHING*
*'The way Ross has utilised light to create a different atmosphere for each image is what really
makes this collection. The soft lighting of dawn is contrasted with the midday luminescence of
the Flower Beetle and the Marigold, highlighting the richly complex characteristics of a British
summer's day.'*

2

3

4

NEIL BYGRAVE
HIGHLY COMMENDED

SPRINGLIFE
1. Male Banded Demoiselle
(Male Banded Demoiselle, *Calopteryx splendens*)
Devon, England

Linking spring and summer, the first sightings of the Male Banded Demoiselle, like a fabulous jewel amid lush new vegetation, is always a wonderful moment, marking the start of the Dragonfly/Damselfly year.

2. Willow Warbler
(Willow Warbler, *Phylloscopus trochilus*)
Devon, England

The male Willow Warbler is captured among fresh gorse blooms. Along with the Chiffchaff, their characteristic song forms an essential element to the uplifting soundtrack of spring.

3. Red Fox Cubs
(Red Fox, *Vulpes vulpes*)
Devon, England

A short break between play fights for two cubs. Their antics shine with the joy of life. Watching them play is always a special spring event.

4. Male Orange-tip Butterfly
(Male Orange-tip Butterfly, *Anthocharis cardamines*, on Cuckoo Flower, *Cardamine pratensis*)
Devon, England

For me, both the Male Orange-tip Butterfly and the Cuckoo Flower are the spring species that ignite the feelings of new life and sheer happiness that is spring.

LIVING LANDSCAPE: CONNECTIVITY

SPONSORED BY

THE WILDLIFE TRUSTS

LIVING LANDSCAPE: CONNECTIVITY WINNER

GRAHAM EATON

Llyn Idwal – War and Peace

Llyn Idwal, Snowdonia, Wales

I was trying to capture an image of the 'complete' landscape of Cwm Idwal. I wanted a different view, one that tells the whole story, not just the stunning view of the mountains and lake surface, with the drama of the weather. In contrast, the peaceful underwater landscape and habitat is rarely seen, but the gin-clear water and algae forests are part of the mountain ecosystem. I have tried to capture the two very different worlds, coexisting, separated by the surface of the lake.

MARK SISSON   HIGHLY COMMENDED

Watching the Starling Roost
(Common Starling, *Sturnus vulgaris*)
Field near Gretna Green, Scotland

On a second consecutive evening visit to photograph the Starling roost near Gretna Green, I came across some birdwatchers wanting to enjoy the experience and spectacle. To increase the sense of scale and the movement in the flock I saw the opportunity to place them in the corner of the frame whilst slowing the shutter speed to achieve the blur of the birds under pressure from a lone Common Buzzard just above the treeline.

PAUL HOBSON   HIGHLY COMMENDED

Orb Spider Living Among Fruiting Lichens
(Orb Spider, *Metellina segmentata*)
Blackamoor Nature Reserve, Sheffield, South Yorkshire, England

Whilst spending a day photographing at Blackamoor Nature Reserve in Sheffield late in the year I came across this Orb Spider among the red fruiting bodies of lichen on an old birch tree. I love the colours and forms of lichens and the spider stayed there for at least three hours as I experimented with compositions.

JACQUI JAY GRAFTON   HIGHLY COMMENDED

Old Friends
(Robin, *Erithacus rubecula*)
East Midlands, England

On early morning walks at Attenborough Nature Reserve, my companion would feed the birds as we walked along, stopping for individual birds and coaxing them down to perch on her hand. This particular robin got to know her very well and would fly down to perch on the front of her mobility scooter. I found this very touching and positioned myself a little way down the path to observe and capture the moment.

DAVID MAITLAND <   HIGHLY COMMENDED

Stubble

(Field Pansy, *Viola arvensi,* Common Field Speedwell, *Veronica persica*)
Feltwell, Norfolk

Field Pansy and Common Field Speedwell reaching towards the light
amongst the stubble of a harvested barley field. Even the most intensely
farmed crops can support wildlife if farming practices are managed – here
the judicious use of herbicides permits the co-existence of wild flowers.

PETER CAIRNS ∧   HIGHLY COMMENDED

The Wow Factor!

(Bottle-nosed Dolphins, *Tursiops truncatus*)
Fortrose, Scotland

The resident pod of Bottle-nosed Dolphins in the Moray Firth are the
world's most northerly and number around 130 animals. Each year as
migrating trout and salmon are flushed up the Firth, crowds gather along
the shoreline to watch these majestic animals hunt. Sometimes the
breaching is so close you can be persuaded that the dolphins are watching
us watching them!

185

DOCUMENTARY
SERIES

DOCUMENTARY SERIES WINNER

NEIL ALDRIDGE

It's Only a Game
(Common Pheasant, *Phasianus colchicus,* Mallard
Duck, *Anas platyrhynchos,* Domestic Dog, *Canis
lupus familiaris)*
Hertfordshire, England

Although I don't shoot, I didn't want to pass up the
opportunity to photograph one of Britain's traditional
country sports. Opinions on country shoots are vastly
polarised. Many people lament the legal hunting of
wild birds like snipe, ducks and woodcock, as well
as the control of indigenous species to protect this
pastime. Others claim that shooting plays a role in
conservation. After all, country pursuits like shooting
have played a major role in saving the last fragments
of Britain's ancient woodland in the last one hundred
years or more. Also, in a world where convenient food
is at our fingertips, it can't be overlooked that this
activity provides its advocates with a connection to
a food source in a way that many have lost. To me,
it is evidence of Britain's long and strange relationship
with nature.

1. A pheasant lies dead in the
leaf litter of an English wood while
a hunter awaits the next drive

2. A spaniel waits, poised, ready to be put into action by its owner to retrieve pheasants shot during a country shoot

3. A male pheasant injured by a shot from a gun is dispatched with a swift blow to the head

5. While pheasants are bred by gamekeepers to be shot, wild birds like woodcock and ducks are also shot on country shoots over the winter months

6. The day's haul – pheasants are paired and strung-up after a country shoot

4. A spaniel retrieves a pheasant shot as part of an English country shoot

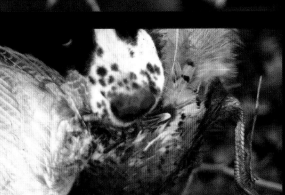

1. Swimming along the monofiliment net we were horrified to find a trapped female basking shark. Initially, we thought she was dead.

2. On being touched, she began to move listlessly. She was exhausted and near death. Her movements disturbed the fine sand, reducing the visibility.

MARK WEBSTER   HIGHLY COMMENDED

Rescue of a Basking Shark From a Bass Net
(Basking Shark, *Cetorhinus maximus*)
Roskilly Cove, Mount's Bay, Cornwall, England

During a survey of eel grass beds for Natural England in Mount's Bay, we came across a bass net deployed in shallow water. As we followed the net we found a young female basking shark trapped in it. Initially we thought the shark was dead, but then noticed she was twitching. Having cut the net away we pulled the shark through the water for several minutes to flow water through her gills and help revive her. Eventually she was able to swim on her own, but initially she turned back towards the net! However, with gentle persuasion she headed back out into the open water of Mount's Bay.

3. We began to cut the net away. Every movement disturbed the seabed, making visibility difficult and photography extremely challenging.

5. With the net clear she lay twitching on her back. We generated a flow of water through her gills, rolled her over and supported her whilst we walked her across the seabed. Eventually she swum slowly and erratically away.

4. Once the net was cut away we peeled it away from the shark. She was lying very still and we feared that we had been too late to save her.

6. Swimming free is how these magnificent fish should be seen. Snorkelling with a basking shark is an awesome experience.

Highland Tiger
(Scottish Wildcat, *Felis sylvestris grampia*)
Cairngorms National Park, Scotland

The Scottish Wildcat is Britain's only surviving native feline and is perilously close to extinction, with an estimated 400 left in the wild. After centuries of persecution and habitat loss, this cultural icon now faces a new threat – that of hybridisation with feral cats. In a country of cat lovers, we are on the brink of losing one of our most charismatic mammals – the Highland Tiger.

1. Illegal persecution remains a threat to the recovery of wildcat numbers
2. A lustrous winter coat equips wildcats for the harsh Highland weather

3. In keeping with other felines, wildcats are surprisingly nimble climbers

5. As traditional wildcat territories are bisected by an expanding road system, casualties are inevitable

4. Establishing genetic purity has until now been possible only through post-mortems. With improving DNA techniques, this is changing rapidly

6. The Scottish Wildcat is an essential ecological component and also a cultural icon, used as an emblem of ferocity and independence

WILDLIFE
ON VIDEO

SPONSORED BY CANON

MARK SISSON

Great Crested Grebe Family
(Great Crested Grebe, *Podiceps cristatus*)
Telford, Shropshire, England

I spent almost the entire spring visiting, photographing and filming this local pair of Great Crested Grebes every morning, nesting on a pool surrounded by houses and busy roads. At face value this was an unpromising site, but the behaviour I was privileged to share with them as they bred, laid and incubated their eggs, brought up their young (which often involved defending random attacks from passing coots) and then escorted them away from the nest area to learn how to fend for themselves, proves the value of looking further at opportunities on your doorstep.

They were so accustomed to my presence each day that at times they would fish around me as I sat filming in the water and reeds and emerge mere feet away, unperturbed, before swimming slowly on about their business. The bond between the two parents and then their chicks showed amazing tenderness at times. It's a spring I won't forget in a hurry.

The full minute video and the commended sequences can be viewed by visiting the BWPA website: www.bwpawards.co.uk

*OUTDOOR
PHOTOGRAPHY
EDITOR'S
CHOICE*

MARK WEBSTER

Nudibranch Grazing on Kelp Frond
(Nudibranch or Sea Slug, *Flabellina pedata*)
Minack Reef, Porthcurno Bay, Cornwall, England

This location is a shallow reef swept by strong tides. In the summer large numbers of Nudibranchs (sea slugs) congregate here on the kelp fronds to feed on the encrusting bryozoans and to mate. They are very small (12-20mm) and must be photographed at high magnification. I used a combination of a wide-angle lens with a teleconverter to capture both the subject and the surface with the sun behind to increase the feeling of depth in the image.

RON PERKINS

**Common Terns Disputing Possession
of a Nest Site**
(Common Tern, *Sterna Hirundo*)
Brownsea Island, Dorset, England

This image was taken from a hide in the Dorset
Wildlife Trust reserve on Brownsea Island. Nesting
was in progress on a crowded island in front of the
hide. Disputes between male terns were frequent.
Sometimes fighting terns flew high; the intensity of this
fight resulted in one tern being driven into the surface
of the lagoon. This image was selected from a long
burst at eight frames per second.

OUTDOOR PHOTOGRAPHY EDITOR'S CHOICE:
APRIL

CATHAL McNAUGHTON

Cormorants Face Crashing Waves
(Great Cormorant, *Phalacrocorax carbo*)
County Antrim coast, Northern Ireland

These cormorants were facing the full force of the waves on a broken and abandoned pier during a storm in the Irish Sea along the County Antrim coast.

DES ONG

Holding-on
(Small White, *Artogeia rapae*)
Loughborough, Leicestershire, England

It was a breezy morning and this little fellow was hanging on for dear life as he got blown from side to side. This head-on shot captures the comical, if a little sorry, look it had while enduring what Mother Nature was throwing at it. Aside from the low light and the continual breeze, the greatest challenge for me was having the patience to wait for the lull to shoot at 1/20th of a second.

YOUNG BRITISH WILDLIFE PHOTOGRAPHERS

Sponsored by

Towergate Camerasure

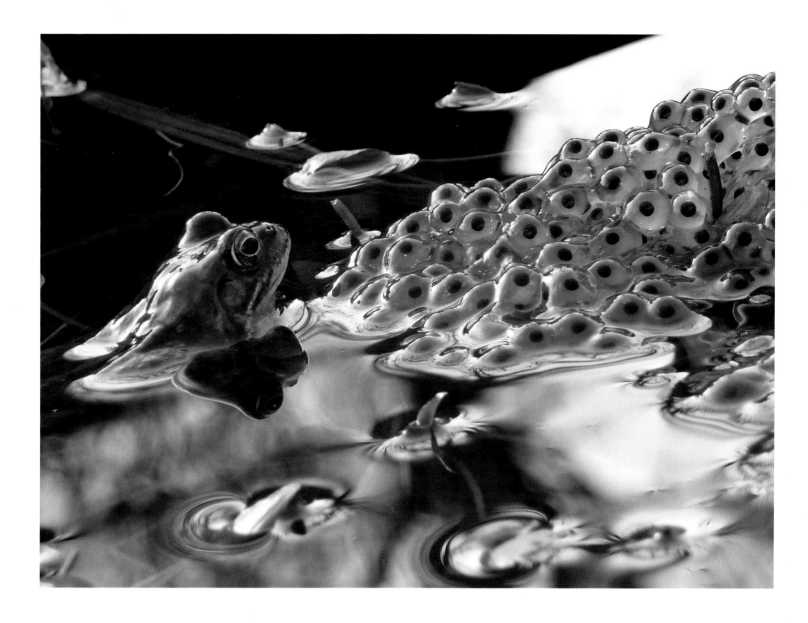

WINNER OF THE UP TO 11 YEARS CATEGORY

WALTER LOVELL (AGE 8) ∧

Frog Checking Its Frogspawn
(Common frog, *Rana temporaria*)
Painswick, Gloucestershire, England

It was a sunny day and I went down to the end of my garden to the pond. I lay down and tried not to scare the frogs. I waited for about 20 minutes and there were about 10 frogs poking their heads in and out of the water. I then saw the perfect picture of a frog and its frogspawn and I took the picture of it.

WINNER OF THE 12 TO 18 YEARS CATEGORY

OLIVER WILKS (AGE 16) >

Red Fox Yawning After His Afternoon Nap
(Red Fox, *Vulpes vulpes*)
Warnham Local Nature Reserve, West Sussex, England

One sunny October afternoon on a trip to Warnham Nature Reserve in Sussex I came across a fox sleeping. Patiently I watched, camera at the ready, waiting for him to wake up. He did and I captured in this shot the moment when he showed me his brilliant white teeth as he yawned and stretched. I think the autumnal lighting compliments the red of the fox, giving great warmth and depth to the image.

LUKE HAWKES (AGE 11)   HIGHLY COMMENDED

Shield Bug on Garden Flower
(Green Shield Bug, *Palomena prasina*)
Woolton, South Liverpool, Merseyside, England

HOLLY PAGET-BROWN (AGE 17)   HIGHLY COMMENDED

Lacewing
(Lacewing, *Chrysopa perla*)
Sevenoaks, Kent, England

JONATHAN FAROOQI (AGE 10)   HIGHLY COMMENDED

Brimstone at Ketton Quarry
(Brimstone Butterfly, *Gonepteryx rhamni*)
Ketton Quarry, Near Ketton, Rutland, England

SAM JACKSON (AGE 14)   HIGHLY COMMENDED

Sloe Bug on a Poached Egg Plant
(Sloe Bug, *Dolycoris baccarum*)
Weeping Cross, Stafford, Staffordshire, England

OSCAR DEWHURST (AGE 16) HIGHLY COMMENDED

Wild Rose Ringed Parakeet in an Apple Tree
(Rose Ringed Parakeet, *Psittacula krameri*)
London, England

JACK BUCKNALL (AGE 15) HIGHLY COMMENDED

Waxwing
(Waxwing, *Bombycilla garrulus*)
Ashington, Northumberland, England

CRAIG McCANN (AGE 16)　　　　　　　　HIGHLY COMMENDED

Ovipositing Emperor Dragonfly
(Emperor Dragonfly, *Anax imperator*)
Teesside, England

ELLA COOKE 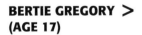   HIGHLY COMMENDED
(AGE 13)

Feed Me!
(Great Tit, *Parus major*)
Buckinghamshire, England

BERTIE GREGORY >   HIGHLY COMMENDED
(AGE 17)

Peregrine Falcon Chicks
(Peregrine Falcon, *Falco peregrinus*)
Vauxhall, London, England

BERTIE GREGORY (AGE 17) ∧ HIGHLY COMMENDED

Squirrel
(Grey Squirrel, *Sciurus carolinensis*)
Regent's Park, London, England

JAMIE UNWIN (AGE 16) > HIGHLY COMMENDED

Red Deer During Late Summer in Pembrokeshire
(Red Deer, *Cervus elaphus*)
Pembrokeshire, Wales

PRELIMS

ROSS HODDINOTT (p.5, 174 – 1)
CAMERA: Nikon D200
LENS: Sigma 150mm macro
SHUTTER SPEED: 1/40
APERTURE: F14
ISO: 200
OTHER: Tripod, remote release

ANDY ROUSE/2020VISION (p.3, 30)
CAMERA: Nikon D3s
LENS: 200-400mm lens
SHUTTER SPEED: 1/400
APERTURE: F6.3
ISO: 800
OTHER: No manipulation

ALEXANDER MUSTARD/2020VISION
(p.9, 161)
CAMERA: Nikon D700
LENS: Sigma 15mm Fisheye lens
SHUTTER SPEED: 1/250
APERTURE: F18
ISO: 1250
OTHER: Underwater housing

DAVE PRESSLAND (p.11, 110)
CAMERA: Nikon D300
LENS: Sigma 150mm f2.8 macro
SHUTTER SPEED: 1/200
APERTURE: F11
ISO: 200
OTHER: Three lens-mounted Nikon SB-R200 speedlights to light the subject and a Nikon SB-800 speedlight on a flash bracket, extended past the subject to light the peony bloom in the background. RAW conversion in Adobe Lightroom, including curves, contrast and vibrance

BWPA 2011 WINNER

RICHARD SHUCKSMITH (p.23, 120)
CAMERA: Nikon D300 in Ikelite housing and twin Inon Z240 strobes
LENS: 10-17mm Tokina fisheye
SHUTTER SPEED: 1/100
APERTURE: F8
ISO: 200
OTHER: The normal manipulation in the way of curves, exposure, tones, saturation etc in lightroom. The clone stamp and healing tool were used in Photoshop to remove backscatter and particles in the water

ANIMAL PORTRAITS

MARK SMITH (p.26)
CAMERA: Canon EOS 7D
LENS: Canon EF 300mm f2.8 IS L
SHUTTER SPEED: 1/640
APERTURE: F3.2
ISO: 800
OTHER: Canon BG-E7, Manfrotto 055CXPRO, Jobu Junior. Processing: Adobe Lightroom 3, Curves, Levels, Sharpening, Noise reduction

ANDY ROUSE (p.27)
CAMERA: Nikon D3s
LENS: 600mm F4 VR with 1.4x teleconverter
SHUTTER SPEED: 1/200
APERTURE: F5.6
ISO: 1000
OTHER: Used beanbag. No manipulation

GRAHAM EATON (p.28)
CAMERA: Nikon D200
LENS: 12-24mm F4
SHUTTER SPEED: 1/125
APERTURE: F11
ISO: 100
OTHER: Underwater housing with two wired strobes. Levels, curves, dust removal, dodge and burn

MARK SMITH (p.29)
CAMERA: Canon EOS 1D Mark IV
LENS: Canon EF 300mm f2.8 IS L
SHUTTER SPEED: 1/1250
APERTURE: F8
ISO: 500
OTHER: Canon EF 2.0x Mark III extender
Technique: Hand-held. Processing: Camera RAW, CS4, Curves, Levels, Sharpening, Noise reduction

STEWARD ELLETT (p.31)
CAMERA: Canon EOS 1D Mark IIn
LENS: Canon 300 IS F2.8
SHUTTER SPEED: 1/200
APERTURE: F2.8
ISO: 320
OTHER: Tripod. Slight Cropping / Standard Saturation – Level Techniques

RON COULTER (p.32)
CAMERA: Nikon 2YS
SHUTTER SPEED: 1/160
APERTURE: F10
ISO: 200
OTHER: Tripod

MATTHEW WATKINSON (p.33)
CAMERA: Canon EOS 20D
LENS: Tamron 18-270mm at 270mm zoom
SHUTTER SPEED: 1/50
APERTURE: F6.3
ISO: 400
OTHER: I had to underexpose the picture to get a shutter speed of 1/50 sec without further increasing the ISO rating so post-processing involved increasing the exposure as well as work on the contrast using curves and the composition by selective cropping

MARK SMITH (p.34)
CAMERA: Canon EOS 7D
LENS: Canon EF 10-22mm f3.5/4.5
SHUTTER SPEED: 1/50
APERTURE: F11
ISO: 200
OTHER: Canon BG-E7, Canon 420EX Speedlite, Stofen diffuser. Technique: Flash -3. Processing: Adobe Lightroom 3, Curves, Levels, Sharpening, Noise reduction

LEE FISHER (p.35)
CAMERA: Canon EOS 1D Mark IV
LENS: 500mm L
SHUTTER SPEED: 1/80
APERTURE: F8.0
ISO: 640
OTHER: Levels and curves adjustment

DES ONG (p.36)
CAMERA: Nikon D700
LENS: Nikon 500mm f4 + 1.4 teleconverter
SHUTTER SPEED: 1/125
APERTURE: F8
ISO: 2000
OTHER: Tripod

BRIAN CHARD (p.37)
CAMERA: Canon EOS 7D
LENS: Canon 500mm f4.5
SHUTTER SPEED: 1/128
APERTURE: F4.5
ISO: 800
OTHER: Beanbag from vehicle window. Levels, curves, hue and saturation, shadows and highlights and clone stamp

AUSTIN THOMAS (p.38)
CAMERA: Canon EOS 1D Mark IV
LENS: Canon 300mm lens
SHUTTER SPEED: 1/1000
APERTURE: F3.5
ISO: 800

OTHER: The camera was tripod-mounted and I manually released the shutter. No filters were used. The image was cropped for composition, levels adjusted and some sharpening and noise reduction applied

TONY MOSS (p.39)
CAMERA: Nikon D3s
LENS: Nikkor 500mm f4 VRII
SHUTTER SPEED: 1/200
APERTURE: F4
ISO: 900
OTHER: Manfrotto tripod, Wimberley BH1 ball-head, Wimberley SideKick, laying flat on the ground to obtain lowest possible viewpoint. Adobe Lightroom/CS5. Curves, USM

RON McCOMBE (p.40)
CAMERA: Canon EOS 7D
LENS: Canon 500mm L IS USM f4
SHUTTER SPEED: 1/250
APERTURE: F6.3
ISO: 320
OTHER: Beanbag on my car window

JAMIE HALL (p.41)
CAMERA: Canon EOS 50D
LENS: Sigma 300mm
SHUTTER SPEED: 1/400
APERTURE: F5
ISO: 200
OTHER: Manfrotto tripod. Colour saturation and sharpened

MARK SISSON (p.42)
CAMERA: Canon EOS 1D Mark IV
LENS: 500mm
SHUTTER SPEED: 1/320
APERTURE: F5
ISO: 200
OTHER: Gitzo tripod, Wimberley head and chest waders. Simple RAW processing in Capture One

JACKY PARKER (p.43)
CAMERA: Nikon D700
LENS: Nikkor 300mm F/2.8
SHUTTER SPEED: 1/500
APERTURE: F10.0
ISO: 400
OTHER: Hand-held. Auto level adjustment made

WILL ATKINS (p.44)
CAMERA: Olympus SP570 UZ 'bridge' type digital camera (12 MP, 26x zoom)
LENS: Olympus ED lens, set at 'Macro' mode
OTHER: No additional equipment – eg filters, tripods etc used; natural light (no flash used). No manipulation used apart from a small cropping of the original image

TERRY WHITTAKER/2020VISION (p.46)
CAMERA: Nikon D3
LENS: Nikon 300 f2.8 lens
SHUTTER SPEED: 1/60
APERTURE: F3.5
ISO: 640
OTHER: Tripod with video head. Hide. LR3, PS CS3, levels, curves

ANDREW PARKINSON (p.47)
CAMERA: Nikon D3s
LENS: 600mmF4 VR lens
SHUTTER SPEED: 1/200
APERTURE: F4
ISO: 400
OTHER: Gitzo tripod, Wimberley head

JULES COX (p.48)
CAMERA: Canon EOS 1D Mark IV
LENS: 300mm f2.8 lens
SHUTTER SPEED: 1/320
APERTURE: F4
ISO: 400
OTHER: Tripod, Wimberley mark II head

JOANNA DAVIES (p.49)
CAMERA: Canon OES 1D Mark IV
LENS: 100mm Macro Lens
SHUTTER SPEED: 1/200
APERTURE: F18
ISO: 200

DES ONG (p.50)
CAMERA: Nikon D700
LENS: Sigma 150mm macro + 1.4 teleconverter
SHUTTER SPEED: 1/1
APERTURE: F16
ISO: 800
OTHER: Tripod

RICHARD PACKWOOD (p.51)
CAMERA: Nikon D3
LENS: Nikkor 500/4
SHUTTER SPEED: 1/250
APERTURE: F4
ISO: 250
OTHER: Beanbags for camera. Fill flash balanced for background ambient light

JULES COX (p.52)
CAMERA: Canon EOS 1D Mark IV
LENS: 300mm f2.8 lens + x 1.4 extender
SHUTTER SPEED: 1/200
APERTURE: F4
ISO: 640
OTHER: Tripod, Wimberley mark II head, angle-finder

STEVE ROUND (p.53)
CAMERA: Canon EOS 7D
LENS: Canon 500mm F4, 1.4x TC
SHUTTER SPEED: 1/640
APERTURE: F6.3
ISO: 320

MATT BINSTEAD (p.54)
CAMERA: Nikon D300s
LENS: AF-S DX VR Zoom-Nikkor 16-85mm
SHUTTER SPEED: 1/1250
APERTURE: F3.5
ISO: 800
OTHER: Minor tweak in contrast

BRETT LEWIS (p.56)
CAMERA: Panasonic Lumix DMC-FT2
SHUTTER SPEED: 1/160
APERTURE: F10
ISO: 200
OTHER: Hand-held in order not to disturb the snake with a tripod

MARK DARLINGTON (p.57)
CAMERA: Canon S90 Powershot
LENS: Compact camera. Set to macro
SHUTTER SPEED: 1/60
APERTURE: Set to programme setting. Auto
ISO: 320

ANIMAL BEHAVIOUR

ANDREW PARKINSON (p.60)
CAMERA: Nikon D3s
LENS: 600mmF4 VR lens
SHUTTER SPEED: 1/800
APERTURE: F5.6
ISO: 200
OTHER: Gitzo tripod, Wimberley head

MARK HAMBLIN (p.62)
CAMERA: Canon EOS 1D Mark IV
LENS: Canon 500mm f4
SHUTTER SPEED: 1/1000
APERTURE: F4.5
ISO: 400
OTHER: Lens resting on beanbag. Stalking technique. Photoshop Curves applied

ANDREW PARKINSON (p.63)
CAMERA: Nikon D3s
LENS: 600mm F4 VR lens and 1.4x converter
SHUTTER SPEED: 1/1250
APERTURE: F5.6
ISO: 800
OTHER: Gitzo tripod and Wimberley head

WENDY BALL (p.64)
CAMERA: Canon EOS 400D
LENS: Canon 100-400mm
SHUTTER SPEED: 1/2000
APERTURE: F5.6
ISO: 400
OTHER: Handheld. Slight adjustment to tone curve using Lightroom 2. Cropped

JOHN OLIVER (p.65)
CAMERA: Canon EOS 5D Mark II
LENS: Canon EF 300mm f4L IS USM. Handheld
SHUTTER SPEED: 1/160
APERTURE: F9
ISO: 400
OTHER: 25mm Kenko Extension Tube. Levels. Curves. Cloned out a small distracting leaf, sharpened image

NEIL BYGRAVE (p.66)
CAMERA: EOS Canon 40D
LENS: Canon 500mm F4 IS L plus 1.4x Extender
SHUTTER SPEED: 1/160
APERTURE: F5.6
ISO: 400
OTHER: Tripod. Evaluative metering -2/3

GLYN THOMAS (p.67)
CAMERA: Canon EOS ID Mark II
LENS: 600 mm lens F4
SHUTTER SPEED: 1/2500
APERTURE: F5.6
ISO: 200

LEE MOTT (p.68)
CAMERA: Nikon D300
LENS: Nikon 500mm F4
SHUTTER SPEED: 1/400
APERTURE: F4
ISO: 1600

PAUL SAWER (p.70)
CAMERA: Canon EOS 1D Mark IV
LENS: Canon 100-400 mm @260mm
SHUTTER SPEED: 1/300
APERTURE: F10
ISO: 125
OTHER: 420 Ex flashgun x3. Off-camera shoe cord 2. Speedlite transmitter ST-E2. Shadow/highlight clone tool to remove debris on water

PHILIP KIRK (p.71)
CAMERA: Canon EOS 5D
LENS: 100-400mm zoom
SHUTTER SPEED: 1/500
APERTURE: F9
ISO: 200
OTHER: Levels, saturation, sharpening

PETER WARNE (p.72)
CAMERA: Canon EOS 7D
LENS: Canon EF 100-400mm L IS at full extension.
SHUTTER SPEED: 1/500
APERTURE: F5.6
ISO: 1600
OTHER: Crop and level adjustments. Removed some food from end of bill with clone stamp

PETER WARNE (p.73)
CAMERA: Canon EOS 7D
LENS: Canon 500mm f4 L + 1.4x converter
SHUTTER SPEED: 1/1000
APERTURE: F6.3
ISO: 1000

OTHER: Beanbag. Very little post-production Reduced high ISO noise a touch, adjusted levels and cropped to balance image

RANA DIAS (p.74)
CAMERA: Nikon D700
LENS: Sigma 150-500mm f/5.6-6.3
SHUTTER SPEED: 1/1000
APERTURE: F6.0
ISO: 200
OTHER: Manfrotto Monopod

THOMAS HANAHOE (p.75)
CAMERA: Canon EOS 1D Mark III
LENS: EF500mm f/4 L IS USM +2.0x
SHUTTER SPEED: 1/800
APERTURE: F8
ISO: 800
OTHER: The RAW image was developed in Photoshop using a variety of techniques

CRAIG CHURCHILL (p.76)
CAMERA: Nikon D3
LENS: Nikon 500 f4 AFS/2
SHUTTER SPEED: 1/400
APERTURE: F7.1
ISO: 1000
OTHER: Beanbag, Nikon TC14E 1.4x conv. Small adjustments in curves

ANDREW PARKINSON (p.77)
CAMERA: Nikon D3s
LENS: 600mm F4 VR lens
SHUTTER SPEED: 1/5000
APERTURE: F4
ISO: 400

DES ONG (p.78)
CAMERA: Nikon D700
LENS: Sigma 150mm macro
SHUTTER SPEED: 1/320
APERTURE: F11
ISO: 1800

THOMAS HANAHOE (p.79)
CAMERA: Canon EOS 1D Mark III
LENS: EF300mm f/2.8L IS USM +1.4x
SHUTTER SPEED: 1/2000
APERTURE: F5.6
ISO: 800
OTHER: The RAW image was developed in Photoshop using a variety of techniques

URBAN WILDLIFE
DAVID BIGGS (p.82)
CAMERA: Canon EOS 40D
LENS: Canon EFL 70-200 F4 Non IS
SHUTTER SPEED: 1/400
APERTURE: F4
ISO: 400
OTHER: Hand-held off of a wooden table behind a garden fence. Lens wide open into sun to create a silhouette

DOUG MACKENZIE DODDS (p.84)
CAMERA: Canon EOS 40D
LENS: 70-200mm L IS F4 set at 200mm
SHUTTER SPEED: 1/800
APERTURE: F4
ISO: 800
OTHER: Exposure bias: +2/3, exposure mode: Aperture priority. Handheld. Cropped in Lightroom

DAMIAN WATERS (p.85)
CAMERA: Canon EOS 30D
LENS: 400mm f/5.6
SHUTTER SPEED: 1/1000
APERTURE: F5.6 -1 fstop
ISO: 400
OTHER: Beanbag support, slight exposure adjustment in Photoshop

MATT SMITH (p.86)
CAMERA: D70
LENS: 18-55mm Nikon
OTHER: Adobe Photoshop used for levels, exposure and colour correction. Also cropped slightly

TERRY WHITTAKER/2020VISION (p.87)
CAMERA: Nikon D3
LENS: Nikon 16-35 f4 lens at 17mm
SHUTTER SPEED: 1/200
APERTURE: F9
ISO: 400
OTHER: Sb800 flashes X 2 in TTL mode, mini tripods, radio camera release. LR3, PS CS3, levels, curves

PAUL HOBSON (p.88)
CAMERA: Canon EOS 5D Mark II
LENS: 16-35
SHUTTER SPEED: 1/3.2
APERTURE: F16
ISO: 1250
OTHER: Beanbag. Flash balanced with lights of the church. Dust specs removed

MICK HOULT (p.89)
CAMERA: Nikon D300s
LENS: Sigma 18-50mm at 50mm
SHUTTER SPEED: 1/13
APERTURE: F13
ISO: 320
OTHER: RAW processed in Aperture. Small levels adjustment, crop and sharpen

BEN HALL (p.90)
CAMERA: Canon EOS 1D Mark IV
LENS: Canon 500mm F4 L IS
SHUTTER SPEED: 1/250
APERTURE: F8
ISO: 400
OTHER: Handheld. Adjusted levels to achieve correct contrast and slight boost in saturation

JAMES SMITH (p.92)
CAMERA: Nikon D3
LENS: Nikon 70-200mm f/2.8
SHUTTER SPEED: 1/50
APERTURE: F3.2
ISO: 800

KEVIN GUTTRIDGE (p.93)
CAMERA: Nikon D80
LENS: 100-300f4
SHUTTER SPEED: 1/2000
APERTURE: F5.6
ISO: 400
OTHER: Cropped

ANDY ROUSE (p.94)
CAMERA: Nikon D3s
LENS: 600mm F4 VR with 1.4x teleconverter
SHUTTER SPEED: 1/320
APERTURE: F5.6
ISO: 1250
OTHER: Beanbag. No manipulation

PAUL HOBSON (p.95)
CAMERA: Canon EOS 1D Mark IV
LENS: 180 macro
SHUTTER SPEED: 1/200
APERTURE: F3.5
ISO: 2500,
OTHER: Compensation -11/3. Tripod. Dust specs removed, slight crop

JAMES SMITH (p.96)
CAMERA: Nikon D3
LENS: Nikon 70-200mm f/2.8 & 1.4 Teleconverter
SHUTTER SPEED: 1/500
APERTURE: F5.6
ISO: 800

HIDDEN BRITAIN
LESLIE HOLBURN (p.100)
CAMERA: Canon EOS 1D Mark III
LENS: EF 100mm F 2/8 MACRO IS USM
SHUTTER SPEED: 1/10
APERTURE: F9
ISO: 1600
OTHER: Monopod

PHIL McLEAN (p.101)
CAMERA: Olympus OM2
LENS: Tamron 90mm Macro
SHUTTER SPEED: 1/60
APERTURE: F11
OTHER: Fuji Sensia200 Slide Film. Benbo tripod, cable release. Scanned slide with Minolta 5400 scanner. Levels,small increase in saturation and sharpened in Photoshop Elements

JOHN H. BRACKENBURY (p.102)
CAMERA: Nikon D300
LENS: Custom-designed, full-frame fish-eye lens with focal length of 2.7mm
SHUTTER SPEED: 1/50
ISO: 200

WILLIAM RICHARDSON (p.103)
CAMERA: Nikon D300s
LENS: 105 F2.8 Nikkor
SHUTTER SPEED: 1/250
APERTURE: F8
ISO: 200
OTHER: Cropped picture for more impact

ALEX WINSER (p.104)
CAMERA: Nikon D300
LENS: Sigma 180mm f/3.5 EX APO Macro IF HSM
SHUTTER SPEED: 1/640
APERTURE: F5.6
ISO: 200
OTHER: Tripod mounted with remote release and mirror lock-up. Minor levels and curves adjustments in post processing

ROSS HODDINOTT (p.105)
CAMERA: Nikon D300
LENS: Sigma 150mm macro
SHUTTER SPEED: 1/0.8
APERTURE: F13
ISO: 160
OTHER: Tripod, remote release, reflector

PHIL McLEAN (p.106)
CAMERA: Canon EOS 1D Mark II N
LENS: Canon 180mm Macro
SHUTTER SPEED: 1/100
APERTURE: F11
ISO: 200
OTHER: Benbo tripod, cable release. Levels, added a little saturation and a small amount of canvas to the left hand side. Sharpened in Photoshop Elements

PAUL HOBSON (p.107)
CAMERA: Canon EOS 1D Mark IV
LENS: 180
SHUTTER SPEED: 1/320
APERTURE: F11
ISO: 800
OTHER: Tripod

JAMIE CRAGGS (p.108)
CAMERA: Nikon D70
LENS: Nikon AF Nikkor28-80mm
ISO: 200
OTHER: Manual flash. Levels, small white dot removed from antennae with clone tool & Unsharpen Mask

ROSS HODDINOTT/2020VISION (p.109)
CAMERA: Nikon D700
LENS: Sigma 150mm macro
SHUTTER SPEED: 1/1250
APERTURE: F6.3
ISO: 200
OTHER: Tripod, remote release

DAN BOLT (p.112)
CAMERA: Olympus E-PL1 PEN
LENS: 8mm fisheye
SHUTTER SPEED: 1/80
APERTURE: F7.1
ISO: 320
OTHER: Olympus underwater housing.
2 x Sea & sea YS110a strobes. Curves adjusted
and slight backscatter removed

MARK WEBSTER (p.113)
CAMERA: Nikon D300
LENS: 105mm micro, 2 x magnifying wet lens
SHUTTER SPEED: 1/200
APERTURE: F32
ISO: 200
OTHER: Subal underwater housing and
amphibious flash guns. Adjusted levels,
colour saturation, unsharp mask, crop

MALCOLM SCHUYL (p.114)
CAMERA: Nikon D300
LENS: Nikon VR 105mm macro
SHUTTER SPEED: 1/60
APERTURE: F22
ISO: 200
OTHER: Camera supported on tripod,
fill flash. Image brightened slightly in Adobe
Photoshop Elements

RACHEL SCOPES (p.115)
CAMERA: Canon EOS 40D
LENS: Sigma 105mm f/2.8 EX DG Macro
SHUTTER SPEED: 1/320
APERTURE: F8
ISO: 250
OTHER: UV filter. Levels to lighten shadows
a little, contrast, and selective sharpening
of ladybird

DES ONG (p.116)
CAMERA: Nikon D700
LENS: Sigma 150mm macro + 1.4 teleconverter
SHUTTER SPEED: 1/10
APERTURE: F16
ISO: 1000
OTHER: Tripod

DANNY BEATH (p.117)
CAMERA: Nikon D80
LENS: Nikkor 55mm micro lens
SHUTTER SPEED: 1/80
APERTURE: F8
ISO: 200
OTHER: Hand-held. Basic adjustments in
photoshop CS2 used, levels, sharpening,
de-spotting and cropping etc, cloudy white
balance selected post capture in raw

COAST AND MARINE
MARCEL VAN BALKOM (p.121)
CAMERA: Canon EOS 1D Mark III
LENS: 70-200 F2.8L USM
SHUTTER SPEED: 1/2500
APERTURE: F4.0
ISO: 500
OTHER: Metering Mode: Center Weighted
Average. Exposure Program: Aperture
Priority. Ai-Servo

ALEXANDER MUSTARD (p.122)
CAMERA: Nikon D300
LENS: Tokina 10-177 Fisheye lens @ 10mm
SHUTTER SPEED: 1/100
APERTURE: F14
ISO: 200
OTHER: Nauticam underwater housing

ANDREW PARKINSON (p.124)
CAMERA: Nikon D3s
LENS: 80-200mm F2.8 lens
SHUTTER SPEED: 1/640
APERTURE: F22
ISO: 800
OTHER: Hand-held

JANE MORGAN (p.125)
CAMERA: Nikon D300s
LENS: 60mm
SHUTTER SPEED: 1/125
APERTURE: F13
ISO: 200
OTHER: Twin Inon Z240 strobes

KRIS WORSLEY (p.126)
CAMERA: Canon EOS 40D
LENS: 17-85mm IS USM @17mm
SHUTTER SPEED: 1/2000
APERTURE: F14
ISO: 100
OTHER: Hand-held. Exposure increased in
Lightroom; shot in landscape orientation and
cropped to portrait

JAMIE CRAGGS (p.127)
CAMERA: Nikon D70
LENS: Nikon AF Nikkor 28-80mm
ISO: 200
OTHER: Manual flash. Auto contrast,
Auto colour & Unsharpen Mask

MATTHEW OXLEY (p.128)
CAMERA: Nikon D200
LENS: NIKKOR 10.5MM F2.8
SHUTTER SPEED: 1/320
APERTURE: F6.3
ISO: 640
OTHER: Sea & Sea DX-D200 Housing and strobe
system. Backscatter was removed from the
image using the 'healing tool' in Photoshop
CS4. A small amount of contrast and a small
amount of sharpening were added

JANE MORGAN (p.130, 131)
CAMERA: Nikon D80
LENS: 60mm
SHUTTER SPEED: 1/100
APERTURE: F13
ISO: 100
OTHER: Twin Sea & Sea strobes

ALEX TATTERSALL (p.132)
CAMERA: Canon EOS 7D
LENS: Tokina 10-17 Fisheye 1.4x Kenko
Pro teleconverter Zen 100mm Dome
Nauticam housing
SHUTTER SPEED: 1/250
APERTURE: F7.1
ISO: 320

ROBERT BAILEY (p.133)
CAMERA: Nikon D300
LENS: Tokina 10 – 17 Fisheye
SHUTTER SPEED: 1/160
APERTURE: F6.3
ISO: 400
OTHER: This picture was taken in 2 metres
of water

ELAINE WHITEFORD (p.134)
CAMERA: Canon EOS 7D
LENS: Canon EF-S 17-85mm,
focal length 28mm
SHUTTER SPEED: 1/100
APERTURE: F14
ISO: 160
OTHER: Ikelite Underwater Housing.
Ikelite DS125 Strobes

MARK WEBSTER (p.135)
CAMERA: Nikon D200
LENS: 18-35mm zoom
SHUTTER SPEED: 1/125
APERTURE: F13
ISO: 100
OTHER: Subal underwater housing and
amphibious flash guns. Adjusted levels,
colour saturation, unsharp mask

ROBERT BAILEY (p.136)
CAMERA: Nikon D300
LENS: Tokina 10 – 17 Fisheye
SHUTTER SPEED: 1/125
APERTURE: F4.0
ISO: 400
OTHER: This picture was taken in 2 metres
of water

DANNY BEATH (p.137)
CAMERA: Nikon D7000
LENS: Micro-nikkor 55mm
SHUTTER SPEED: 1/80
APERTURE: F8
ISO: 200
OTHER: Polarising filter used. Basic adjustments
in photoshop CS2 used, levels, sharpening,
de-spotting and cropping etc

RICHARD SHUCKSMITH (p.138)
CAMERA: Nikon D3
LENS: 200-400mm F4 Nikkon
SHUTTER SPEED: 1/640
APERTURE: F6.3
ISO: 500
OTHER: Normal manipulation curves, exposure,
saturation etc, all done in lightroom

LEE MOTT (p.139)
CAMERA: Nikon D300
LENS: Nikon 400mm 2.8
SHUTTER SPEED: 1/1600
APERTURE: F4.5
ISO: 400

ALEXANDER MUSTARD/2020VISION (p.140)
CAMERA: Nikon D700
LENS: Sigma 15mm Fisheye lens
SHUTTER SPEED: 1/160
APERTURE: F14
ISO: 640
OTHER: Subal underwater housing. 2 x Inon
underwater flashguns

ANDREW PARKINSON (p.141)
CAMERA: Nikon D3s
LENS: 80-200mm F2.8 lens
SHUTTER SPEED: 1/400
APERTURE: F16
ISO: 800
OTHER: Hand-held

THOMAS HANAHOE (p.142)
CAMERA: Canon EOS 1D Mark III
LENS: Canon EOS 24-70mm F2.8 L @24mm
SHUTTER SPEED: 1/2000
APERTURE: F5.6
ISO: 500
OTHER: The image was captured in the Raw
format and developed in Photoshop

CHRISTINE ROBERTS (p.143)
CAMERA: NIKON D200
LENS: NIKON 60mm macro
SHUTTER SPEED: 1/200
APERTURE: F20
ISO: 200
OTHER: Sea & Sea underwater housing,
Inon strobes. Minor exposure, levels and
saturation adjustments

WILDLIFE IN MY BACKYARD
RANA DIAS (p.146)
CAMERA: Nikon D700
LENS: Sigma 150mm f/2.8 Macro
SHUTTER SPEED: 1/250
APERTURE: F5.6
ISO: 200
OTHER: Hand-held

RON COULTER (p.148)
CAMERA: Nikon D700
LENS: Sigma 50-500
SHUTTER SPEED: 1/2000
APERTURE: F6.3
ISO: 1600
OTHER: Tripod

THOMAS HANAHOE (p.149)
CAMERA: Canon EOS 1D Mark IV
LENS: Canon EOS 17-40mm F4 L @ 34mm
SHUTTER SPEED: 1/5000
APERTURE: F4
ISO: 3200
OTHER: The image was captured in the Raw
format and developed in Photoshop

CHARLES EVERITT (p.150)
CAMERA: Canon EOS 40D
LENS: Canon 500mm IS
SHUTTER SPEED: 1/500
APERTURE: F4
ISO: 400
OTHER: Beanbag. Levels and saturation adjusted

CHRIS GRABSKI (p.151)
CAMERA: Nikon D90
LENS: Nikkor 18-105 mm
SHUTTER SPEED: 1/80
APERTURE: F7.1
ISO: 100
OTHER: 3 extension tubes:12, 20 & 36. CS3,
Camera RAW 4.6, Adjustment layers, High Pass
Filter + Mask, very limited cloning

ALBEL SINGH (p.152)
CAMERA: Canon EOS 550D
LENS: EF100mm f/2.8L Macro IS USM
SHUTTER SPEED: 1/125
APERTURE: F13
ISO: 1250

MARK HAMBLIN (p.153)
CAMERA: Canon EOS 1D Mark IV
LENS: Canon 500mm f4
SHUTTER SPEED: 1/320
APERTURE: F8
ISO: 400
OTHER: Tripod. Photoshop Shadows and
Highlights applied

MARK HAMBLIN (p.154)
CAMERA: Canon EOS 1D Mark IV
LENS: Canon 500mm f4
SHUTTER SPEED: 1/1300
APERTURE: F5.6
ISO: 400
OTHER: Camera mounted on tripod. Taken from
wooden hide. Photoshop Curves applied

HABITAT

IAN PAUL HASKELL (p.158)
CAMERA: Canon EOS 1D Mark IV
LENS: 500mm f4 L
SHUTTER SPEED: 1/500
APERTURE: F4
ISO: 400
OTHER: Car used as a hide. Curves, capture sharpening. Slight crop to the top of the image to suit panoramic format. Increased black by 5

BEN HALL (p.159)
CAMERA: Canon EOS 1D Mark IV
LENS: Canon 17-40mm L
SHUTTER SPEED: 1/250
APERTURE: F13
ISO: 250
OTHER: Gitzo tripod. Adjusted levels to achieve correct contrast and slight boost in saturation

BEN HALL (p.160)
CAMERA: Canon EOS 1D Mark II
LENS: Canon 100-400mm L IS
SHUTTER SPEED: 1/0.5
APERTURE: F29
ISO: 50
OTHER: Gitzo tripod and mirror lockup. Adjusted levels to achieve correct contrast and slight boost in saturation

CHINCH GRYNIEWICZ (p.162)
CAMERA: Fuji FinePix S2Pro
LENS: Sigma 14mm f 2.8
SHUTTER SPEED: 1/125
APERTURE: F9.5
ISO: 100
OTHER: Basic conversion of raw file in Photoshop CS2

MARK HAMBLIN (p.164)
CAMERA: Canon EOS 1D Mark IV
LENS: Canon 17-40mm @ 21mm
SHUTTER SPEED: 1/100
APERTURE: F11
ISO: 400
OTHER: Hand-held crawling along the cliffs on my stomach inching to within 30cm of this bird that duly obliged by flapping his wings. Photoshop Highlights and Shadows applied

BEN HALL (p.165)
CAMERA: Canon EOS 1D Mark IV
LENS: Canon 500mm L
SHUTTER SPEED: 1/80
APERTURE: F5.6
ISO: 250
OTHER: Gitzo tripod. Adjusted levels to achieve correct contrast and slight boost in saturation

MARK N THOMAS (p.166)
CAMERA: NIKON D3
LENS: Sigma 15mm fisheye
SHUTTER SPEED: 1/40
APERTURE: F6.3
ISO: 1250
OTHER: Twin Sea and Sea 110 strobes, set on minimum

CHRIS O'REILLY (p.167)
CAMERA: Canon EOS 1D Mark IV
LENS: 500mm
SHUTTER SPEED: 1/160
APERTURE: F5.6
ISO: 400
OTHER: Tripod

ELLIOTT NEEP (p.168)
CAMERA: Canon EOS 1DS Mark II
LENS: 16-35mm l at 35mm
SHUTTER SPEED: 1/320
APERTURE: F10
ISO: 200

OTHER: Camera resting on beanbag on a car door. Image received contrast correction to foreground and minimal exposure correction to sky

GREG MORGAN (p.169)
CAMERA: Canon EOS 7D
LENS: Canon 500mm f4
SHUTTER SPEED: 1/800
APERTURE: F4
ISO: 200
OTHER: Basic processing – increased kelvin, colour saturation, contrast etc

DES ONG (p.170)
CAMERA: Nikon D700
LENS: Tamron AF 28-75mm XR Di
SHUTTER SPEED: 1/40
APERTURE: F2.8
ISO: 6400
OTHER: Tripod

GRAHAM STOKES (p.171)
CAMERA: Nikon D300
LENS: Fish Eye Lens
SHUTTER SPEED: 1/125
APERTURE: F11
ISO: 200
OTHER: I used 4xSB800, two inside and two outside the trunk. I used a beam camera trigger to capture the image at the right time. Some Levels, Curves and saturation

BRITISH SEASONS

ROSS HODDINOTT (p.175 – 2)
CAMERA: Nikon D300
LENS: Sigma 150mm macro
SHUTTER SPEED: 1/30
APERTURE: F7.1
ISO: 100
OTHER: Tripod, remote release

ROSS HODDINOTT (p.175 – 3)
CAMERA: Nikon D700
LENS: Sigma 150mm macro
SHUTTER SPEED: 1/1250
APERTURE: F2.8
ISO: 200
OTHER: Tripod, remote release

ROSS HODDINOTT (p.175 – 4)
CAMERA: Nikon D300
LENS: 150mm
SHUTTER SPEED: 1/320
APERTURE: F5.6
ISO: 100
OTHER: Tripod, remote cord

NEIL BYGRAVE (p.176 – 1)
CAMERA: Canon EOS 50D
LENS: Canon 300mm F4 L IS plus 1.4x Extender
SHUTTER SPEED: 1/200
APERTURE: F9
ISO: 400
OTHER: Tripod. Evaluative Metering -1/3

NEIL BYGRAVE (p.176 – 2)
CAMERA: Canon EOS 7D
LENS: Canon 500mm F4 L IS plus 1.4x Extender and Canon Extension Tube EF 25 II
SHUTTER SPEED: 1/1000
APERTURE: F6.3
ISO: 320
OTHER: Tripod. Evaluative Metering -1

NEIL BYGRAVE (p.176 – 3)
CAMERA: Canon EOS 7D
LENS: Canon 500mm F4 L IS plus 1.4x Extender
SHUTTER SPEED: 1/500
APERTURE: F5.6
ISO: 400
OTHER: Tripod. Evaluative Metering +2/3

NEIL BYGRAVE (p.177 – 4)
CAMERA: Canon EOS 7D
LENS: Canon 300mm F2.8 L IS plus 2 x Extender and Canon Extension Tube EF 25 II
SHUTTER SPEED: 1/160
APERTURE: F13
ISO: 320
OTHER: Fill Flash -3, Tripod. Evaluative Metering -1

LIVING LANDSCAPE: CONNECTIVITY

GRAHAM EATON (p.180)
CAMERA: Nikon D200
LENS: 10.5mm
SHUTTER SPEED: 1/8
APERTURE: F20
ISO: 160
OTHER: Tripod, ND grad, underwater housing 2 wired strobes. Curves, ND grad, dust removal, dodge and burn, water droplets removed from housing port

MARK SISSON (p.181)
CAMERA: Canon EOS 1DS Mark II
LENS: 24-70mm at 70mm
SHUTTER SPEED: 1/10
APERTURE: F2.8
ISO: 400
OTHER: Gitzo tripod and Wimberley head. Simple RAW processing in Capture One

PAUL HOBSON (p.182)
CAMERA: Canon EOS 1D Mark IV
LENS: 180
SHUTTER SPEED: 1/10
APERTURE: F16
ISO: 500
OTHER: Tripod. By keeping low I could get some warm light from the tree's leaves in the corner of the background

JACQUI JAY GRAFTON (p.183)
CAMERA: Nikon D3X
LENS: Nikon 300mm f2.8 VR
SHUTTER SPEED: 1/20
APERTURE: F10
ISO: 100
OTHER: Hand-held

DAVID MAITLAND (p.184)
CAMERA: Canon Powershot G11
LENS: Set at 6.1mm, macro setting
SHUTTER SPEED: 1/200
APERTURE: F5.6
ISO: 80

PETER CAIRNS (p.185)
CAMERA: Canon EOS 1D Mark II
LENS: 500mm lens
SHUTTER SPEED: 1/1000
APERTURE: F4
ISO: 200

DOCUMENTARY SERIES

NEIL ALDRIDGE (p.188-189)
CAMERA: Canon EOS 1D Mark III
LENS: Canon EF 50mm f1.8 II
SHUTTER SPEED: 1/80
APERTURE: F10
ISO: 800

MARK WEBSTER (p.190-191)
CAMERA: Nikon D100 (Images 1-5) Nikon D200 (Image 6)
LENS: 12-24mm zoom
SHUTTER SPEED: 1/40
APERTURE: F9
ISO: 200
OTHER: Subal underwater housing and amphibious flash guns. Adjusted levels, colour saturation, unsharp mask

PETER CAIRNS (p.192-193)
CAMERA: Canon EOS 1 Mark IIn and 5D bodies
LENS: 17-500mm Canon lenses
OTHER: Gitzo tripods

WILDLIFE ON VIDEO

MARK SISSON (p.196-199)
CAMERA: Canon EOS 1D Mark IV
LENS: A combination of 70-200mm, 500mm and 600mm lenses along with 1.4x converter
OTHER: Supported by a very stable Gitzo tripod and Kirk Ballhead and made possible by a good pair of chest waders

OUTDOOR PHOTOGRAPHY EDITOR'S CHOICE

MARK WEBSTER (p.202)
CAMERA: Nikon D300
LENS: 10-17mm fish eye zoom and 2x teleconverter
OTHER: Subal underwater housing and amphibious flash guns. Adjusted levels, colour saturation, unsharp mask

RON PERKINS (p.203)
CAMERA: Nikon D700
LENS: Nikon 200-400mm f4.0 + 1.4x TC
SHUTTER SPEED: 1/1600
APERTURE: F9.0
ISO: 400
OTHER: Hand-held. Adjusted in Levels and Curves, cropped

CATHAL McNAUGHTON (p.204)
CAMERA: Canon EOS 1D Mark IV
LENS: Canon 400mm f2.8
SHUTTER SPEED: 1/12
APERTURE: F28
ISO: 400

DES ONG (p.205)
CAMERA: Nikon D300
LENS: Sigma 150mm macro
SHUTTER SPEED: 1/20
APERTURE: F11
ISO: 400
OTHER: Tripod, reflector

YOUNG BRITISH WILDLIFE PHOTOGRAPHERS

WALTER LOVELL (p.208)
CAMERA: Panasonic Lumix, DMC TZ5
SHUTTER SPEED: 1/80
APERTURE: F4.8

OLIVER WILKS (p.209)
CAMERA: Canon EOS 50D
LENS: Sigma 150-500mm
SHUTTER SPEED: 1/320th
APERTURE: F6.3
ISO: 400

Index

Photographers' Websites

NEIL ALDRIDGE www.conservationphotojournalism.com

WILL ATKINS www.lehart.org

ROBERT BAILEY www.robertbaileyphotography.com

DANNY BEATH www.flickr.com/photos/flickering_velvet

DAVID BIGGS www.biggsphotography@tiscali.co.uk

MATT BINSTEAD www.mattbinstead.blogspot.com

DAN BOLT www.underwaterpics.co.uk

JOHN H. BRACKENBURY www.seingsmall.com

NEIL BYGRAVE www.naturelens.co.uk

PETER CAIRNS www.northshots.com

CRAIG CHURCHILL www.craigchurchill.co.uk

JULES COX www.julescoxphotography.co.uk

MARK DARLINGTON www.twistedimages.co.uk

JOANNA DAVIES www.joannadaviesphotography.co.uk

RANA DIAS www.aprishot.com

GRAHAM EATON www.eatonnature.co.uk

STEWARD ELLETT www.eyesofthewild.co.uk

CHARLES EVERITT www.charleseveritt.com

LEE FISHER leefisherwildlifephotography.co.uk

CHRIS GRABSKI www.members.photoportfolios.net/chrishg

CHINCH GRYNIEWICZ www.chinch-gryniewicz.com

KEVIN GUTTRIDGE www.naturalsurroundings-photography.com

BEN HALL www.benhallphotography.com

MARK HAMBLIN www.markhamblin.com

THOMAS HANAHOE www.hanahoephotography.com

PAUL HOBSON www.paulhobson.co.uk

ROSS HODDINOTT www.rosshoddinott.co.uk

MICK HOULT www.naturalhistoryimages.co.uk

JACQUI JAY GRAFTON www.jacquijay.com

BRETT LEWIS www.brettlewisphotography.co.uk

DOUG MACKENZIE DODDS www.dmackdimages.co.uk

DAVID MAITLAND www.davidmaitland.com

RON McCOMBE www.wildlife-photography.uk.com

PHIL McLEAN www.philmclean-photography.co.uk

GREG MORGAN www.gregmorganphotography.co.uk

JANE MORGAN www.morganreefphotography.com

TONY MOSS www.tonymosswildlife.com

LEE MOTT www.imagesinnature.co.uk
www.leemottphotography.co.uk

ALEXANDER MUSTARD www.amustard.com

ELLIOTT NEEP www.neepimages.com

JOHN OLIVER www.johnoliverphotography.co.uk

DES ONG www.desong.co.uk

MATTHEW OXLEY www.photographymatthewoxley.wordpress.com

JACKY PARKER www.jackyparker.com

ANDREW PARKINSON www.andy@andrewparkinson.com

DAVE PRESSLAND www.btinternet.com/~pressland/dave

WILLIAM RICHARDSON www.wrphotographic.com

STEVE ROUND www.stevenround-birdphotography.com

ANDY ROUSE www.andyrouse.co.uk

PAUL SAWER www.paulsawer.co.uk

MALCOLM SCHUYL www.wildvisions.co.uk

RACHEL SCOPES www.flickr.com/photos/rachel_s

RICHARD SHUCKSMITH www.ecologicalphotography.co.uk
www.earthinfocus.com

ALBEL SINGH www.flickr.com/photos/albelsingh

MARK SISSON www.marksissonphoto.co.uk
www.natures-images.co.uk

JAMES SMITH www.jswp.org

MARK SMITH www.marksmithphotography.net

MATT SMITH www.mattsmithimaging.com

GRAHAM STOKES www.naturalapertuer.com
www.grahamstokesphotography.com

ALEX TATTERSALL www.uwvisions.com

MARK N THOMAS www.marknthomasimages.co.uk

AUSTIN THOMAS www.austin-thomas.co.uk

GLYN THOMAS www.glynthomas.com

MARCEL VAN BALKOM www.natuurfoto.biz
www.marcelvanbalkom.nl

PETER WARNE www.flickr.com/Peter-EppingForest

DAMIAN WATERS www.drumimages.co.uk

MATTHEW WATKINSON www.fishsnorkel.com

MARK WEBSTER www.photec.co.uk

ELAINE WHITEFORD www.sublimescubaphotography.com

TERRY WHITTAKER www.terrywhittaker.com

OLIVER WILKS www.oliverwilksimages.co.uk

ALEX WINSER www.alexwinserphotography.co.uk

KRIS WORSLEY www.krisworsley.com